Microeconomic
Issues
of the 70s

MICROECONOMIC ISSUES OF THE 70s
Exercises in Applied Price Theory

KATHARINE C. LYALL

Johns Hopkins University
Center for Metropolitan Planning & Research

Harper & Row, Publishers
New York, Evanston, San Francisco, London

Sponsoring Editor: John Greenman
Project Editor: Eleanor Castellano
Designer: Michel Craig
Production Supervisor: Robert A. Pirrung

Library of Congress Cataloging in Publication Data
Lyall, Katharine.
    Microeconomic issues of the 70s.
    1. Microeconomics—Problems, exercises, etc.
I. Title
HB171.5.L94   338.973   73–13303
ISBN 0–06–044117–8

Contents

Contents

Preface

This is a collection of elementary and intermediate exercises in the application of microeconomic theory to contemporary issues designed to supplement a standard textbook or to be employed as examination questions. It is not a drill book in the ordinary sense since I have taken care to avoid mere repetition of mathematical and graphic manipulations and have concentrated instead on combining concepts within a problem so the student sees (1) what the ideas mean in the context of a specific case, (2) how they fit together to give an analysis of a case, (3) how an analysis can be used to support a policy conclusion, and (4) if one does not care for the conclusion, on what grounds the underlying conditions may be legitimately attacked and the results revised.

Few students will retain the details of microtheory long after the course is completed. What may be expected, however, is a lasting understanding that economic reasoning is a branch of "moral philosophy," that its conclusions are reasoned from premises, and accordingly that the results of economic analysis are neither to be accepted as infallible technical answers nor to be brushed aside as mere opinion. To master the process of logical argument about economic policies is to acquire the ability to be relevant and hard-minded about decisions that affect the quality of economic and social existence, present and future.

For this reason, and because they are the most prominent contemporary economists raising the broader issues of a satisfactory economic system, I include questions based on the writings of Milton Friedman and John Kenneth Galbraith. The problems in this collection are so constructed as to minimize the amount of writing and reading required and maximize the amount of thinking time available for a complete answer. Ideas are linked together to bring the student, by steps, to a logical conclusion. To get a complete answer he must see not only the individual pieces but also their interrelation to form the whole analysis.

I have deliberately selected topics on which some journal literature exists so that students interested in particular issues can, if they're so inclined, follow up the references supplied in the notes. References are abbreviated in the notes as follows: *American Economic Review* (AER), *Journal of Political Economy* (JPE), *Quarterly Journal of Economics* (QJE), *Southern Economic Journal* (SEJ), *Western Economics Journal* (WEJ), and the *Journal of the American Institute of Planners* (JAIP).

The mathematical competence required is no more than high school algebra; though a few problems may be solved more quickly with calculus, none requires this approach. A glossary of common mathematical and graphic relationships is provided at the end of the book. Questions involving more advanced mathematical and theoretical concepts are marked with an asterisk and can easily be omitted without sacrificing the main line of argument. A hint to the user: All graphs appearing in problems are drawn to scale. You will find it useful to be as accurate as possible in working with these since some answers may be read directly from the diagrams.

My thanks to John Hagens for checking both questions and answers in detail, to Anne Blalock for typing the manuscript, and to numbers of my students at Cornell and Syracuse Universities who have used and suggested improvements in many of the exercises included here.

KATHARINE C. LYALL

KEY TO APPROPRIATE CHAPTERS IN MICROECONOMICS TEXTS

[specific page numbers shown in ( )] [Becker's lecture numbers indicated by #]

Problem Number	Becker[1]	Bilas[2]	Clower & Due[3]	Ferguson[4]	Kogiku[5]	Leftwich[6]	Levenson & Solon[7]	Mansfield[8]	Nicholson[9]	North & Miller[10]	Shows & Burton[11]	Watson[12]
1	2, 5, 6-#19	2 (15)	3, 8	4, 8	3	3	3, 8	4	6, 14	3	2, 4	2, 3, 13, 14
2	2, 5, 6-#19	2	3, 8	4, 8	3	3	3, 8	4	6, 14	—	2, 4	2, 3, 13, 14
3	2, 5, 6-#19	2	3, 8	4, 8	3	3	3, 8	4	6, 14	—	2, 4	2, 3, 13, 14
4	2, 5, 6-#19	2	3, 8	4, 8	3	3	3, 8	4	6, 14	—	2, 4	2, 3, 13, 14
5	2, 5, 6-#19	2	3, 8	4, 8	3	3, 10 (235)	3, 8	4	6, 14	—	2, 4	2, 3, 13, 14
6	6-#19 (91)	2 (31)	8 (175)	—	3 (82)	—	3 (45)	8 (240), 12 (357)	14 (286)	—	—	13 (279)
7	3-#11	3	4, 5	2	1	4	4	2	7 (109)	—	3	4
8	3-#11	3	4, 5	2	1	4	4, 12	2	3, 4, 26	—	3	4
9	3-#11	3	4, 5	2	1	4	4	2	3, 4, 26	—	3	4
10	3	4	4, 5	2, 3	1	5	5	2, 3	5	—	3	5
11	3	4, 11 (282), 5	4, 5	2, 3	1	5	5, 12	2, 3, 12 (345)	5	—	11, App.	5 (113)
12	3	4	4, 5	2, 3	1	5	5	2, 3	5	—	3	5
13	7	4	5, 6	16	2, 4	—	15	14 (406)	12	—	13	10
14	—	4 (68)	—	15 (430)	—	5 (90)	9 (190)	2 (42)	20 (406)	—	3	15
15	5-#15	7	6	7	—	8	7	6, 12 (348)	12	11	5	8
16	5	7	6, 11	7	5	8	7	6	12	—	5	11
17	6, 7	7, 8, 9	6, 8, 9	7, 8, 9	3, 5	8, 9, 10	7, 8	6, 7, 8	14, 15	—	5, 7	8, 11, 13, 14, 16
18	6-#20	9	6, 8, 9	9	5	*10	9	9	15	—	8	4 (76), 16
19	6-#22	5 (97), 9	9	9	5	10	9	9 (272)	15 (296)	—	8	4 (76), 17
20	6-#22	5 (97), 9	9	9	5	10	9	9 (272)	15 (296)	—	8	17
21	6-#20, 22	9	9	9	5	10	9	—	15	9, 25	8	17

	[1]	[2]	[3]	[4]	[5]	[6]	[7]	[8]	[9]	[10]	[11]	[12]
22	6–#20	9	9	9	5	10	9	9	15	—	8	16
23	6–#20	9	9	9	5	10	9	9 (272)	23	—	13	17
24	—	11 (292)	12	14	5	14 (307)	11 (240), 12	13 (367)	17 (342), 18	—	10	22
25	6–#21, 22	10	11	11	5	11	10	11	16	—	9	19
26	6–#21, 22	10	11	11	5	10, 11 (217)	10	11	16	—	9	19
27	6–#21, 22	—	11	11	2, App. (258)	—	—	11 (313)	9 (146) (159)	—	—	20 (451)
28	—	—	2, 16	—	—	—	—	16	10	—	—	20
29	6–#21	10	11	11	—	(242)	10 (205)	11	16	—	9	19 (424)
30	9	—	4, 5	2, 13	1	16	4, 12, 15	12, 15 (413)	7 (114), 26	29, 30	3, 11	4 (81), 22
31	4	5 (109)	—	1	—	—	—	—	9 (149)	—	—	7 (142)
32	—	—	—	—	2	—	1	—	—	2, 17, 18, 27	—	—
33	5–#16	11 (285)	13 (375)	13 (375)	—	13 (295)	12 (351)	17 (332), 19 (377)	—	—	11	21 (471)
34	—	12	16	—	4	17	13, 15	15	23, 25	19, 28	13	15
35	—	12	16	—	4	17	13, 15	6 (157), 15	22 (442), 23, 25	14, 20	13	15
36	—	12	16	—	4	17	13, 15	6 (157), 15	22 (442), 23, 25	14	13	15
37	—	12	16	—	4	17	13, 15	15	20, 21, 23	22	13	15
38	—	12	16	—	4	17	13, 15	15	21, 23	—	13	15
39	—	12	16	—	4	17	13, 15	15	23, 24	—	13	10 (214)
40	—	5 (94)	3 (70)	—	—	—	—	3 (72)	5 (92)	—	—	—
41	—	5 (94)	3 (70)	—	—	—	—	3 (72)	5 (92)	—	—	—
Glossary	—	—	—	—	—	—	—	—	—	2, 8 (136)	—	—

[1] Gary Becker, Economic Theory (New York: Knopf, 1971).
[2] Richard A. Bilas, Microeconomic Theory (New York: McGraw-Hill, 1971).
[3] Robert W. Clower and John F. Due, Microeconomics, 2d ed. (Homewood, Ill.: Irwin, 1972).
[4] C. E. Ferguson, Microeconomic Theory, rev. ed. (Homewood, Ill.: Irwin, 1969).
[5] K. C. Kogiku, Microeconomic Models (New York: Harper & Row, 1971).
[6] Richard H. Leftwich, The Price System and Resource Allocation, 4th ed. (Hinsdale, Ill.: Dryden Press, 1970).
[7] Albert M. Levenson and Babette S. Solon, Essential Price Theory (New York: Holt, Rinehart & Winston, 1971).
[8] Edwin Mansfield, Microeconomics (New York: Norton, 1970).
[9] Walter Nicholson, Microeconomic Theory (Hinsdale, Ill.: Dryden Press, 1972).
[10] Douglass C. North and Roger L. Miller, The Economics of Public Issues, 2d ed. (New York: Harper & Row, 1973).
[11] E. Warren Shows and Robert H. Burton, Microeconomics (Lexington: Heath, 1972).
[12] Donald S. Watson, Price Theory and Its Uses, 3d ed. (Boston: Houghton Mifflin, 1972).

PART I.
Market demand, consumer behavior, and static equilibrium

A. Demand theory and equilibrium

1. Operation intercept—the market for an illicit good

In September, 1969 the U.S. government instituted intensive searches for marijuana at the Mexican border. Officials reasoned that a decrease in supply would raise the price out of reach of most users and that since marijuana is not addictive this would not result in an increase in criminal activity to finance the higher prices. Figure 1 (page 4) shows the estimated marijuana market before Operation Intercept.

P_m/lb	Market for Heroin Q_d (when P_h/lb = $1000)
$ 50	19
100	14
150	17
200	19
250	20

1. Explain briefly what changes in market conditions you would expect to result from the crackdown (assuming it

is successful), and show these, where possible, on the diagram. Would you expect the new equilibrium emerging from these changes to be stable or unstable?

2. In its argument as stated here, what implicit assumption is the government making about the price elasticity of demand for marijuana? Is this correct? (Prove your answer.) What would you expect to be the long-run result of the government's assumption in these circumstances?

3. Calculate the cross-elasticity of demand between marijuana and heroin when the price of marijuana jumps from $150 to $250 per pound. Explain what this tells you.

By December, 1969 the U.S. government had to admit that despite its search and seizure operations at the Mexican border the price of marijuana had not increased much in the United States. Suppose now that in an effort to discourage

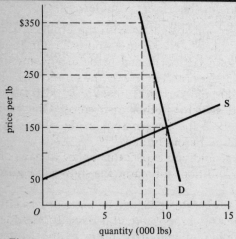

Figure 1. U.S. Marijuana Market

organized crime syndicates from entering the business a new proposal is made to legalize marijuana but to levy a tax on it, similar to those on liquor and cigarettes, so as to keep the price out of reach of casual users.

Your senator votes against the proposal, giving the following reasoning:

> The effect of a tax on a commodity might seem at first sight to be an advance in price to the consumer. But an advance in price will diminish demand, and reduced demand will send the price down again. It is not certain, therefore, that the tax will really raise the price.

4. Write the senator a letter explaining the error in his reasoning, and illustrate your point graphically. (Be concise. Remember, the senator is a busy man.)

5. Give your own *economic* reasoning for supporting or opposing the new proposal. Note: For this purpose assume that your own objective is to reduce the use of marijuana by keeping the price high.

6. Six months later, still struggling with the problem, the government decided to try another approach. On June 30, 1971 it announced that it had made arrangements with the Turkish government to buy the entire Turkish poppy crop and to pay certain bonuses to Turkish farmers who would switch to other cash crops. One year later, in June, 1972 the government made similar arrangements to buy heroin in Laos.[2]

   a. What effect would you expect this policy to have on the market conditions for marijuana shown in Figure 1?

   b. Would you expect this policy to be more or less efficient than the tax proposal (had it passed) in reducing the number of marijuana users in the United States? (You may want to distinguish long-run from short-run effects here.)

NOTES

1. Actual prices for marijuana reported for the market at Syracuse University for the 1970–1971 academic year in L. Kramer, "The Grass and Hash Business at Syracuse University," *Fortune* (September, 1971): 102–103. There is a strong seasonal pattern in the demand for marijuana, peaking during the examination periods in January and May; the yearly range is $125–170 per pound. Profits for on-campus distributors in that year averaged about 50 percent of initial cash investment by dealers. See also S. Rottenberg, "The Clandestine Distribution of Heroin, Its Discovery and Suppression," *JPE* 76, 1 (January, 1968): 78–90.

2. B. Gwertzman, "The Flow Is Endless," *New York Times*, August 20, 1972, p. E2.

2. Sic transit gloria mundi (or, what to do about public transit?)

You, the mayor of New York, are concerned about a deficit in the New York City transportation budget. Your advisors recommend an increase in the subway fare from 35c to 45c to cover the deficit, but your political sense tells you that this might cause some public reaction in the form of a partial boycott of the subway system. The only information you have to go on in making your decision is the following:

Subway Fare	Number of Subway Rides Taken	Number of Bus Rides Taken*
10c	1500	1200
20c	1300	1400
30c	1100	1600
35c	1000	1700
40c	900	1800
45c	800	1900
50c	700	2000
60c	500	2200
70c	300	2400

*Bus Fare = 45c.

(Assume that the City owns both bus and subway lines but sets their fares separately. Assume further that the subway system has no serious capacity problem.)

1. Explain the logic of the calculation necessary to reach a decision.
2. Show your calculation and result.
3. What specific changes in the use of transit facilities can you expect to occur as a result of an increase in the subway fare from 35c to 45c?
   a. What can you say about the specific relationship between bus and subway transportation in New York City? Prove your point mathematically.
   b. Does your mathematical result support what you would have intuitively guessed about the bus-subway relationship? If not, how can you explain the difference?
   c. Will the cross-elasticity of demand for bus rides with respect to subway fares ($E_{b,s}$) be the same as the cross-elasticity of demand for subway rides with respect to bus fares ($E_{s,b}$)?
4. Draw a double-decker diagram showing the demand for and total revenue from subway services. (Be sure that the diagrams are accurately aligned vertically.) Referring to your diagram, explain briefly the correct policy to pursue in closing the deficit.[1]
*5. The discussion so far has assumed that the subway authority charges a *single price* equal to the average cost per person-trip in order to break even. Looking at the situation now from the rider's viewpoint, compare the average cost per trip by subway with his average cost per trip by private automobile as he switches more and more of his trips from public transit to private automobile. (Assume that he already owns an automobile.)
   a. How can this be used to explain the evident "underuse" of public transit and "overuse" of private automobiles in U.S. cities?[2]

b. What effect do you think the use of a differentiated subway fare (higher fares during rush hours than at other times) might have on
1) The total number of subway rides?
2) The average cost per person-trip of subway operation?
3) The distribution of rides throughout the day?[3]

NOTES

1. The classic study of this problem is W. Vickrey, *The Revision of the Rapid Transit Fare Structure of the City of New York* (New York Finance Project, Technical Monograph #3, 1952). A more up-to-date report is W. Lassow, "Effect of the Fare Increase of July 1966 on the Number of Passengers Carried on the New York City Transit System," *Highway Research Record*, 213 (1968): 1–7.

2. See also R. Sherman, "A Private Ownership Bias in Transit Choice," *AER 57*, 5 (December, 1967): 1211–1217 and reprinted in D. S. Watson, *Price Theory in Action*, 2d ed. (Boston: Houghton Mifflin, 1969), pp. 319–324.

3. For related problems involving intermodal choice and the use of public transit subsidies, see L. Moses and H. Williamson, Jr., "Value of Time, Choice of Mode, and the Subsidy Issue in Urban Transportation," *JPE 71*, 2 (June, 1963); A. Altshuler, "Transit Subsidies: By Whom, for Whom?" *JAIP 35*, 2 (March, 1969): 84–89; and G. Kraft and T. Domencich, "Free Transit," in M. Edel and J. Rothenberg, eds., *Readings in Urban Economics* (New York: Macmillan, 1972), pp. 459–480.

3. Bouzy Rouge in the American market

Georges Vesselle, a French wine maker and mayor of the village of Bouzy, recently announced that he intends to market in the United States a red champagne called Bouzy Rouge.[1] Since he is unfamiliar with the American market, you are hired to advise him on proper U.S. marketing strategy. Your re-

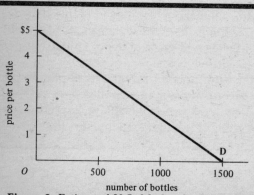

Figure 2. Estimated U.S. Market for Bouzy Rouge

search produces the demand curve for red champagne shown in Figure 2.

1. M. Vesselle informs you that he expects his grape crop in the coming year to yield 1000 bottles of champagne. Draw the supply curve on the diagram.
2. What is the price elasticity of supply for the short run? Will this be the same, less than, or greater than the price elasticity of supply in the long run?
   How would you define the length of the "short run" in this case?
3. Using data from the diagram, give the specific equation for the demand curve: Q_d = _____.
4. At what price would you advise M. Vesselle to enter the American market next year?
5. Show on the diagram the effect of a telegram bearing the bad news that unseasonal hailstorms have cut the expected grape crop in half.
   a. Will the new equilibrium be stable or unstable?
   b. Will the quantity *demanded* at the new equilibrium be more, less, or equally as price elastic as that demanded at the original equilibrium point? (Give your reasoning.)
   c. Will this telegram cause you to make any change in your marketing recommendations to M. Vesselle? Explain.
6. Suppose that your market research indicates that demand for Bouzy Rouge (i.e., the Q demanded at each P) in the United States will grow at about 10 percent per year over the next five years.
   a. What will be the price of a bottle of Bouzy Rouge next year if your research is accurate?
   b. Will this long-term expectation have any effect on your marketing recommendations for next year? Explain.

NOTES

1. *New York Times*, September 26, 1971, p. 20.

4. Subsidy and profit in the market for news

At many schools the student newspaper is subsidized by the school out of student fees and distributed free on campus. This procedure is criticized by some students, who don't like to have their fees used in this way; by some administrators, who don't like the editorial views; by some faculty, who decry the generally low quality of student reporting and writing; and by some citizens of the local community, who distrust student publications in general. Suppose that a decision is made to try to overcome some of these objections by having the *Student News* "go commercial"—that is, charge for its issues and, if possible, make a profit. It must at least break even, since no more subsidies will be forthcoming.

1. Using data from Figure 3, give the specific equation for the demand and supply curves:

   $Q_d =$ _____ $Q_s =$ _____

2. What are the *ceteris paribus* conditions for the *supply* curve?

3. What was the original equilibrium price and quantity (under the subsidy)?

4. What is the equilibrium price and quantity necessary to keep the "new" *Student News* in business? Will this equilibrium be stable or unstable?

5. What must have been the minimum amount of the subsidy from the university in past years?

6. Show on the diagram and explain briefly in a sentence or two the effect you would expect from the following events:

   a. The student assembly votes to give $2000 from the portion of student fees over which it has discretionary control to the campus literary magazine.

   b. The university raises tuition (but not fees). For a given price, will the new demand curve resulting from the tuition change be more, less, or equally as elastic as the original demand curve? Give your reasoning.

7. The presumption against the compulsory financing of student programs from general fees implied in the case just examined has been applied to a wide variety of student services ranging from athletic passes to yearbooks.

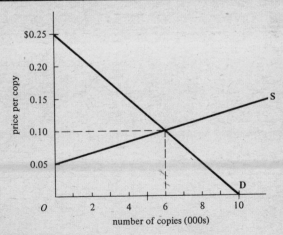

Figure 3. Market for Student Newspaper

Such programs, it is argued, should make their way on voluntary sales and contributions or disappear.

On what basis would you determine which, if any, student programs should be funded collectively by fees paid to the university and which by voluntary contributions?

5. The pricing of Broadway hits

The demand for tickets to a "smash" Broadway show is presented in Figure 4.

1. Complete the lower diagram. (Make sure that it is properly aligned vertically with the top diagram.)
2. What are the *ceteris paribus* assumptions of the demand curve?
3. Explain why the demand curve slopes downward. Do you think this is a correct representation? Why or why not?

   Why are no cost curves shown? Are these necessary to determine the profit-maximizing price for the theater to charge? Explain.
4. Use the diagrams to show what would be the proper pricing policy for the theater to use. (Assume that only one price can be charged for all seats.)

   Explain the profit-maximization rule used and why it works (i.e., why following the stated rule does in fact maximize profits).

   At what price and quantity should the theater operate?

5. Calculate the price elasticity of demand for theater tickets at the present price of $12. (Note: You will need to write down the specific equation for the demand curve.)

   a. If the theater has only 550 seats, what is the best pricing policy? (Compare this with your answer to question 4.)

   b. Suppose that the theater can rent and install extra seats at an average cost of $2 each per performance. How many, if any, should be installed and what should the ticket price be after expansion of the seating capacity?

   c. If the theater installs no extra seats but instead raises its price to $15, the practice known as "scalping" (re-

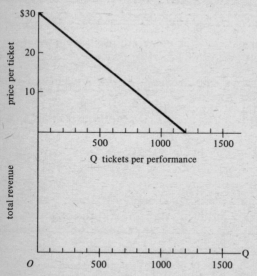

Figure 4. Demand and Total Revenue from the Sale of Tickets to a Broadway Hit
(Q = tickets per performance)

sale of tickets for prices higher than box office prices)
will be observed.

Explain why this will happen. Is scalping an undesirable practice for the theater? for the public?

6. The theater manager, concerned about the potential effects on his business of a new 4 percent income tax (to
be levied on all incomes *earned* in New York City),
receives the following telegram from his consulting
economist at Princeton:

$$\Delta Q/Q \cdot \Delta Y/Y = 1.20$$

Explain what it says and interpret for the manager what
it implies for the future of his business.[2]

NOTES

1. Charles Nelson, in the "Puzzles and Problems" section of
JPE 80, 2 (May/June, 1972): 620, points out that scalping is illegal in
New York City but legal in London; it is even facilitated by London
theaters, which lend space on their premises to professional resale
agents. Does this mean that one of these theaters is failing to follow
a profit-maximizing price policy?

2. For a detailed discussion of U.S. theater pricing problems, see
W. Baumol and W. G. Bowen, *Performing Arts: The Economic Dilemma*
(New York: Twentieth Century, 1966).

B. Comparative static adjustment

6. Professional cobwebs

In the early 1960s there was a great deal of concern in the United States about a "shortage" of engineers, scientists, college teachers, and other extensively trained professionals. In the 1970s this shortage has apparently become a "surplus," with unemployment rates in these professions among the highest in the country. Enrollments in engineering and Ph.D. programs are declining as students switch to training in other fields with more promising employment prospects. Employers in these fields have expressed concern about what appears to be a cyclical pattern of periodic over- and undersupply of highly trained personnel in these professions.[1]

Static theory tells us that short-term shortages will be eliminated in the long run by a rise in price that elicits greater supply. But when there is a lag in the "production" process due to extended training time, the *path* of adjustment may be cyclical, converging, diverging, or perpetually oscillating around an equilibrium.

1. Define a market shortage in the *static* sense. Is it possible to have a long-run shortage, or is this by definition a short-run phenomenon?

Figure 5(a) is a diagram of conditions in the market for engineers. Note that the demand and supply curves are "dated"; that is, the subscripts indicate that D is for year t while the S curve shows quantities that will be supplied in the *following* period (t + 4), four years later, in response to *this* period's prices (salaries). If we assume that individuals determine the kind of training they will undertake with an eye to present salaries, we can use the cobweb theorem and the diagram to analyze the cyclical pattern of shortage and surplus of engineering skills.[2]

2. The cobweb theorem describes a process of *dynamic* adjustment of price and quantity toward their equilibrium levels.

   a. Mark the equilibrium price and quantity, P_0Q_0. Is this a stable or an unstable equilibrium?

   b. Starting from P_1, Q_1, show on the diagram the movement of price and quantity toward the equilibrium point, marking each period's price P_2, P_3, P_4, etc.
   How many periods will it take for this equilibrium to be reached?

   c. The length of the period (time lag) between S and D decisions is shown on the diagram as four years. What reason can you think of for this? What difference would it make if the time lag were reduced to two years?

   d. Plot in Figure 5(b) the time path of the price movements you traced out in question 2b.
   Is this a converging, diverging, or perpetually oscillating price pattern?

   e. What determines whether the cycle will be converging, diverging, or perpetually oscillating?[3]
   What would the relationship between the relative

slopes of the S and D curves have to be to produce a convergent price pattern if S and D curves applied to the *same* time period?

3. The cobweb pattern describes movements around a particular equilibrium point, *ceteris paribus*. Suppose now that the end of the Vietnam War leads to disarmament and a general cutback in government research and construction expenditures.

   a. What effect would this have on the relationships shown in the diagram?
   b. What effect would this have on the cyclical pricing pattern analyzed in question 2 above?
   c. Suppose that the demand for engineers becomes perfectly inelastic.
      1) Draw the new D curve on the diagram.

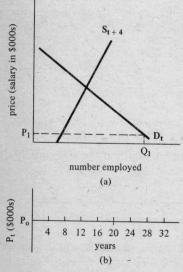

Figure 5. (a) Market for Engineers.
(b) Time Path of Price Adjustments

2) What effect, if any, would this have on the long-run price adjustment of engineers' salaries?

3) What effect, if any, would it have on the long-run supply of engineering skills?

4. Cobweb analysis was originally used to explain cyclical movements in the prices of agricultural products.[4] It might be assumed that as the economy became increasingly industrialized the problem of cyclical prices would become increasingly insignificant. J. K. Galbraith argues that a conspicuous feature of modern U.S. industry is the long lead times required for planning, developing, and marketing technologically sophisticated products. What does this suggest about the future importance of price instabilities in the United States?

5. Most practicing (and potential) engineers would agree that cyclical fluctuations in the salaries of engineers, as described earlier, have an undesirable effect both on individuals' incomes and on the long-run supply of these skills. What actions can you think of that might be taken to stabilize the cycle?

6. Comment on this view:

All the current talk about a "surplus" of engineers is economic nonsense; it is simply a roundabout way of saying that these professionals refuse to work for their market price, insisting on the higher salaries of earlier years when demand conditions were different. There is no such thing as a surplus of skills from society's standpoint.

NOTES

1. "Engineers: 'Help Wanted' Again," *New York Times*, March 11, 1973, p. E9.

2. For a different explanation in terms of dynamic shifts in demand, see K. J. Arrow and W. M. Capron, "Dynamic Shortages and Price Rises: The Engineer-Scientist Case," *QJE 73*, 2 (May, 1959): 292–308, reprinted in Watson, *op. cit.*, pp. 352–362.

3. You should be able to determine the precise mathematical conditions using your diagram and the equations for the supply and demand curves.

4. For an application of cobweb analysis to agricultural production, see A. A. Harlow, "The Hog Cycle and the Cobweb Theorem," *Journal of Farm Economics 42*, 4 (November, 1960): 842–853), excerpts from which are reprinted in Watson, *op. cit.*, pp. 164–168.

C. Consumer theory—cardinal utility

7. Cram session—a familiar allocation problem

Suppose that you wake up tomorrow to discover that you have 12 hours of study time in which to prepare for three exams. For each hour of study you can expect your grades to be as follows:

Hour	Exam A	Exam B	Exam C
1	40	60	30
2	65	90	46
3	80	100	60
4	90	100	72
5	95	90	82
6	99	75	90
7	100	55	96
8	100	33	100
9	99	8	100
10	95	.0	100

Naturally you want to allocate your time so as to maximize your total (numerical) score on all three exams. (Each is weighted equally in your cumulative average.)

1. Calculate the marginal utility of each hour of study for each exam. (List your results beside the total scores in the table.)
2. Draw diagrams for total utility and marginal utility for each exam. (Be sure that they are accurately aligned vertically.) Assume that the scores given are what you will have "earned" at the *end* of each hour of study. Plot MU at the end of the hour in which it was earned.
3. State briefly the meaning of negative marginal utility in this example.
4. State the general rule you should follow to divide your time so as to maximize your total score on all three exams.

   Applying this, how many hours should you devote to each exam?

   A = —————— B = —————— C = ——————
5. How many hours should you spend on each if you have *unlimited* study time?

   A = —————— B = —————— C = ——————

   if you have only *five* hours?

   A = —————— B = —————— C = ——————

   (You need your diagram to answer this.) Explain your procedure briefly.
6. Should you change your allocation of study time if grades are recorded not numerically but in letters with the following numerical equivalents: A = 90–100, B = 80–89, C = 70–79, D = 60–69, F = 0–59, and the following grade-point equivalents: A = 4.0, B = 3.0, C = 2.0, D = 1.0, F = 0? (Assume that no plus or minus grades are used.)

   Under this system of letter grading, how should you allocate your time if you have
   a. Unlimited study time?

      A = —————— B = —————— C = ——————
   b. Only five hours available?

      A = —————— B = —————— C = ——————
   c. Twelve hours available?

      A = —————— B = —————— C = ——————

7. Considering what you now know about both grading systems, would you prefer letter or numerical grading? What factors weigh in your judgment on this besides the time requirements you've worked out?

   In your opinion is the allocation process spelled out in detail here a realistic general description of the way students actually allocate their study time?[1]

NOTES

1. For an interesting interpretation of the significance of the marginal utility of time in modern consumption patterns, see S. B. Linder, *The Harried Leisure Class* (New York: Columbia University Press, 1970).

8. Income distribution in a collective Utopia

Suppose that, disillusioned with the individual competitive scramble to keep up with the Joneses, you join a cooperative utopian commune whose motto is: "The greatest total utility for the community as a whole." In this commune everyone works at something, and income is pooled and distributed to members each week.[1]

1. How should the commune's total income of $100 be divided among its ten members to be consistent with its philosophy? (Give the allocation rule and explain in common-sense terms *why* it gives maximum total utility.)
2. On what *assumptions* does your answer to question 1 rest?
   a. Does the allocation rule you've just used in question 1 imply that each member's share must be the same, or is it possible that under some circumstances the individual shares will be unequal?
   What assumptions are necessary to ensure that equal shares will maximize total utility?

   b. Does the successful application of your allocation
      rule require the assumption that everyone's utility
      from money (income) is the same? Why or why not?
3. In your opinion is the allocation rule of question 1 a practical one (i.e., can it be applied in practice or is it only of
   theoretical value)? Indicate what information you
   would need to apply it and/or suggest a more practical
   alternative allocation rule.
4. Would the allocation rule used in question 1 be an
   equally good guide to maximize total utility if:
   a. The $100 were donated from outside sources instead
      of earned by members of the commune?
   b. The total to be allocated were $100 of tax liabilities
      instead of income?

NOTES

1. One of the first and most interesting American utopian com-
munities based on cooperative production was founded by Robert
Owen in New Harmony, Indiana. New Harmony was essentially an
agricultural commune patterned after an industrial community
founded earlier by Owen in Scotland. For an account of the found-
ing and subsequent failure of New Harmony, see J. F. C. Harrison,
Robert Owen and the Owenites (London: Routledge & Kegan Paul,
1969) and O. C. Johnson, ed., *Robert Owen in the United States.*
(New York: Humanities Press, 1970).

9. The economics of financial aid

Suppose that you are empowered by the dean of admissions to allocate $500,000 among 1000 applicants for financial aid, including incoming freshmen. The dean is anxious to maximize the total utility to the school of awards from the scholarship fund.

1. By what rule should you allocate the money?
2. What assumptions would you have to make about the recipients?
3. What factual information, if any, would you need to have about the applicants?
4. Explain in utility terms why you might want to consider a student's academic average in this allocation procedure.
5. Explain briefly to the dean why
   a. Total utility will be less if he requires you to favor children of alumni in your allocation.
   b. Total utility will rise if he can get a wealthy alumnus to donate an additional $10,000 to the scholarship

fund, even though those who receive grants from this money may not derive as much utility from them as earlier recipients of financial aid.

6. In your opinion would the allocation resulting from the rule you've specified be "fair" as well as efficient? Be sure to explain how you define *fair* in your answer.[1]

NOTES

1. For an examination of the efficiency and equity aspects of state-subsidized university education in California, see S. A. Hoenack, "The Efficient Allocation of Subsidies to College Students," *AER 61*, 3, P. I (June, 1971): 302–311.

D. Consumer theory—ordinal utility

10. Awards—incentives at what price?

It is common practice for colleges to give awards at the end of the academic year for excellence in a variety of endeavors ranging from sports to overall academic performance. The award may take a number of forms: a citation, medal, or letter; some item of value such as books; or simple cash.

Suppose that you have just been notified by the dean that you have won a college book award. This consists of $20 worth of books selected for the student by the nominating faculty member. Figure 6 is an indifference map showing your preferences between books and cash and your present budget line. Use this information to analyze the award from the standpoint of its cost to the college and its efficiency in providing incentive for academic excellence.

1. What is the economic interpretation of the slope of the budget line?
2. What is your equilibrium combination of books and cash (before you receive the award)?

3. Does this indifference map show increasing or decreasing marginal utility for books? Explain. (Think carefully about this.)

4. Show on the diagram the effect of receiving the book award, and mark the new equilibrium point A.

Suppose now that the treasurer suggests that the college could give the same incentive and reward for excellence with less expense if it gave cash instead of books.

5. Show on the diagram the effect of a cash award that would provide the same incentive and reward as the current book award, and mark the new equilibrium point B.

6. How much cash would the committee have to give you to equal the book award?
   Is the treasurer right—*is* cash cheaper?

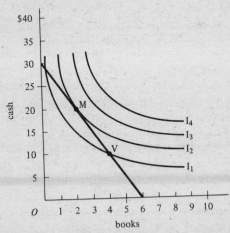

Figure 6. Indifference Map and Budget Line of Recipient Before Award Is Made

7. Finally, show on the diagram the result of a committee decision to continue to make the award in the form of books but to allow the *student* to select them himself.
8. Conclusion: Should the committee make the award in the form of books or money if it wants
   a. To provide maximum incentive and reward for scholarship?
   b. To economize on the college budget?

Issues in the War on Poverty

A federal drive against poverty begun under the Johnson administration and dubbed the War on Poverty has produced a variety of antipoverty programs and proposals ranging from minor alterations and extensions of the existing welfare system (closer policing of eligibility rolls, more food stamps, public housing, etc.) to the scrapping of the present system and the substitution of a guaranteed minimum income (the "negative income tax"). Some politicians have taken the view that welfare payments should be firmly tied to an obligation to work on public projects or other employment provided by the state; others argue that the administrative costs of policing present welfare programs and eligibility are excessive and that direct cash payments on the basis of federally reported income would be more efficient and less demeaning than compulsory work programs and most present grant programs.

In the following problems you are asked to analyze first the economic effects and then the probable social effects of two basic choices in poverty programs: (1) the choice between employment subsidies and a guaranteed minimum income, and (2) the choice between cash grants and specific aid programs such as food stamps or housing assistance.

11. The working poor—wage subsidies or guaranteed minimum income?

Examination of the 20 percent of the U.S. population currently classified as receiving incomes below the officially defined
poverty level has revealed that a substantial proportion are
employed, that they are "working poor." Figure 7 is the budget
line and indifference map for an unskilled worker who is one
of the working poor (i.e., he is employed, but his income is
below the poverty level).

1. What is his equilibrium combination of income and
   leisure? Why is this an equilibrium?
2. What is the economic interpretation of the slope of the
   budget line?
3. The government is considering two alternative policies:
   I. Pay a wage subsidy to employers who hire such
      workers at the minimum wage of $2 per hour (the
      subsidy to equal the difference between $2 and the
      current wage paid to those workers).
   II. Pay a cash grant directly to the worker that would
      give him the same total utility as policy I.

a. Show the effect of policy I on the diagram and label the new equilibrium combination of income and leisure A.
b. Show the effect of policy II on the diagram and label the new equilibrium point B.
c. Using the equilibrium combinations of income and leisure indicated at points A and B, indicate on your diagram the income and substitution effects of Policy I (the wage subsidy) on the amount of *leisure* chosen by the worker. (Letter any additional points as necessary.)

   Does this indicate that leisure is a "normal" or an "inferior" good in the eyes of this particular worker?

4. Which policy gives the greatest incentive to work (i.e., to give up leisure)? Prove this with reference to the diagram.

5. What is the cash cost to the government of each alternative? (Read from the diagram.)

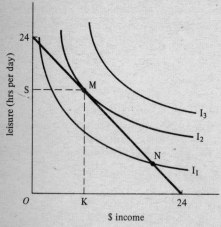

Figure 7. Budget Line and Indifference Map for One of the "Working Poor"

6. Using these results, evaluate a politician's comment that "We will save the taxpayers' money and the workers' dignity by giving wage subsidies to encourage more work instead of cash handouts."[1]

NOTES

1. Another alternative policy might be a negative income tax to be paid to individuals whose incomes fall below some specified level, regardless of whether they are working or not. A Negative Income Tax Experiment funded by the Office of Economic Opportunity and designed to test the labor supply response was carried out in New Jersey and Pennsylvania from 1968 to 1971; other experiments are currently under way in Seattle, Denver, Gary, and rural North Carolina. See M. J. Boskin, "The Negative Income Tax and the Supply of Work Effort," *National Tax Journal 20*, 4 (December, 1967): 353–367; P. A. Diamond, "Negative Taxes and the Poverty Problem," *National Tax Journal 21*, 3 (September, 1968): 288–303; A. J. Heins, "The Negative Income Tax, Head Grants, and Public Employment Programs: A Welfare Analysis," *Journal of Human Resources 5*, 3 *(Summer 1970)*: 298–303; E. K. Browning, "Alternative Programs for Income Redistribution: The NIT and the NWT," *AER 63*, 1 (March, 1973): 38–49; and J. Kesselman, "Conditional Subsidies in Income Maintenance," *WEJ 9*, 1 (March, 1971): 1–20. Progress reports on the field experiments are found in the American Economic Association *Papers and Proceedings 61*, 2 (May, 1971): 15–68.

12. Rent subsidies, public housing, or cash grants?

Strategists in the War on Poverty have commonly proposed programs to subsidize certain necessities of life such as food and shelter for people with incomes beneath the poverty line. The mechanics vary from coupon systems such as food stamps to construction of public housing to be rented at less than market rates. In this problem you are asked to analyze a choice between a cash grant and two kinds of housing programs:

I. A federal public housing program in which apartments are constructed by the government and offered to eligible poverty candidates at rents below market rates on a take-it-or-leave-it basis (i.e., if the recipient refuses public housing he receives no other housing assistance).

II. A rent subsidy program in which the recipient locates and chooses his own housing in the commercial market and the federal government pays 50 percent of the rental price.

Figure 8 is the budget line and indifference map for an individual receiving $200 per month in cash under our current welfare system before any housing assistance program has been adopted.

1. What is the economic interpretation of the slope of the budget line?
2. Show on the diagram the effect of the 50 percent rent subsidy. (Hint: Ask yourself whether this is an income or a relative-price change.)

   Letter additional points on the diagram as required in answering the following series of questions:

   a. Label the new equilibrium point for the recipient X. Label the new quantity of housing chosen H.
   b. How much would it have cost him in terms of cash (i.e., value of other goods) to purchase H amount of housing without a rent subsidy?

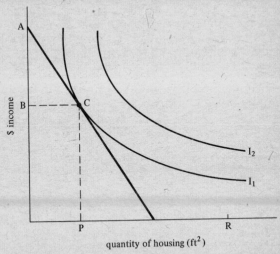

Figure 8. Indifference Map and Budget Line for Individual Welfare Recipient Before Housing Assistance

   c. What is the amount of rent subsidy that would have to be paid for H under program II?

3. Now show on the diagram how much *cash* the government would have to give the recipient to make him as well off as he would be under the rent subsidy. (Note: This would be a cash grant not tied to his rent or any other specific expenditure.)

   a. Label this new equilibrium point E.
     Label the corresponding quantity of housing G.

   b. Why does the equilibrium combination of housing and other goods (cash) vary with different payment schemes, even though both combinations (X and E) give the same total utility?

   c. How much will it now cost the recipient in cash for H amount of housing if he pays for it at market prices out of a cash grant instead of with a rent subsidy?

4. Now you are in a position to compare the cost of providing H amount of housing to the recipient under a rent subsidy with the cost of providing it through a cash grant. Make this comparison by filling in the following table with the relevant quantities specified on your diagram:

COST OF PROVIDING H AMOUNT OF HOUSING WITH

	Rent Subsidy	Cash Grant
Government's cost		
Recipient's cost		
Total cost		

   a. Which program is costlier to the government? to the recipient?

   b. Which program has the greatest total cost?

   c. The difference between the costs to the government of the two programs is a measure of the cost to the taxpayer of imposing the donors' preferences on the recipient. Explain.

Judging from your diagram, would you say that the cost of imposing the donors' preferences in housing programs is a large or a small percentage of the total cost of a given housing program? On what does this depend (look at your diagram)?

5. Consider now the public-housing program under which the federal government would construct apartments R square feet in size and offer them on a take-it-or-leave-it basis to eligible recipients at 50 percent of the commercial market rent. (This is a combination of subsidized rent and a preselected quantity of housing space to be consumed.)

   a. What would be the cost per apartment of this program to the government?

   b. How does this public-housing program compare with the rent subsidy program as an efficient means of raising the recipient's total utility?

   Will this always be true, or is the efficiency of public-housing programs in raising utility just a matter of finding the "correct" (efficient) size of apartment (larger or smaller than R)?[1]

6. You have now examined three possible programs: (1) rent subsidy, (2) public housing, and (3) cash grants. Summarize your conclusions in the following way:

   a. Which program is the most efficient (i.e., increases utility per dollar of cost most, or costs the least to achieve a given utility level) for the government? Which is the next most efficient? Which is the least efficient?

   b. Which program will raise the average standard of housing (measured in square feet of space) most? next? least?[2]

   c. Which program do you think would be easiest and cheapest to administer fairly and humanely?

d. What other factors might you want to consider in choosing one of these three types of housing programs?[3]

7. Would you now agree or disagree that "Transfers in kind are always less efficient instruments than direct cash grants for achieving an increase in welfare for the poor"?[4]

NOTES

1. See H. J. Aaron and G. M. von Furstenberg, "The Inefficiency of Transfers in Kind: The Case of Housing Assistance," *WEJ 9*, 2 (June, 1971): 184–191 on this point.

2. H. O. Nourse, "The Effect of a Negative Income Tax on the Number of Substandard Housing Units," *Land Economics 46*, 4 (November, 1970): 435–446.

3. For a related analysis of a food stamp program, see R. Bilas, *Microeconomic Theory: A Graphical Analysis,* 2d ed. (New York: McGraw-Hill, 1971), pp. 86–87.

4. For discussions of this view see M. Friedman, *Capitalism and Freedom* (Chicago: Phoenix, 1962), pp. 178–180; E. Smolensy, "Public Housing or Income Supplements—The Economics of Housing for the Poor," *JAIP 34*, 2 (March, 1968): 94–101; and R. Bish, "Public Housing: The Magnitude and Distribution of Direct Benefits and Effects on Housing Consumption," *Journal of Regional Science 9*, 3 (December, 1969): 425–438.

13. Bread and beer on a student budget—the importance of the optimal mix

1. Use the following data to construct a budget line and an indifference map for an average college student.

Indifference Curve		Budget Data	Production Possibility Curve	
Bread	Beer	The average student		
35	70	has a budget of $30	0	50
40	50	per month. Bread	25	45
45	40	costs $0.33 per loaf	37½	40
52½	30	and beer costs $2.50	52½	30
85	20	per six-pack.	67½	10
			70	0

2. What explains the shape of the indifference curve?
3. What is the marginal rate of substitution involved in going from 20 to 30 units of beer? _____ from 30 to 40? _____ from 40 to 50? _____ Compare this with the marginal rate of substitution involved in going from 50 to 40 units of beer, from 40 to 30, and from 30 to 20.

4. What is the relative price of bread in terms of beer? _____ of beer in terms of bread? _____
5. What is the equilibrium composition of goods the student should purchase to maximize his total utility?
6. State the technical (mathematical) condition that identifies the consumer's equilibrium point.
7. Suppose that the relative price of bread in terms of beer becomes 8:5. Show the effect on your diagram and specify the new equilibrium point: _____ units of bread and _____ units of beer.

Suppose now that the indifference map you've drawn represents the collective preferences of the entire college community.

8. On what underlying assumptions does the community indifference map depend? Are these assumptions different for an individual's indifference map?
9. Plot the community production possibility curve on your diagram. What is the community equilibrium composition of output: _____ units of beer and _____ units of bread.
   What is the marginal rate of transformation involved in going from 20 to 30 units of beer? from 30 to 40? from 40 to 50? (Compare this with your answer to question 3 above.)
10. Show on your diagram the effects of an overall change in society's tastes in favor of beer.
11. What is the *law of diminishing marginal utility*? How is it reflected in an indifference curve?

14. Edgeworth exchange at midnight

Indifference maps can be used to analyze the optimal distribution of goods among individuals and the conditions of exchange between them. Although the following problem is defined for two individuals, keep in mind that the same analysis can be applied to two countries or two government agencies exchanging fixed amounts of goods and services.[1]

Suppose that you purchase a pizza from the only pizza parlor in town just before it closes. When you get it home you discover that you are out of beer! However, your next-door neighbor is studying late and happens to have two six-packs of beer in his refrigerator to fortify him for the long night ahead. Clearly the possibility of some form of exchange should be explored. Your preferences are reflected in Figure 9, a double indifference map known as an Edgeworth box diagram.

1. Initially you have all the pizza and he has all the beer available to both of you. Mark the point on the diagram corresponding to these initial conditions A.

2. Now suppose that you offer to trade four slices of pizza for three bottles of beer. Label the point at which such an exchange would place you B.
   a. Is this a rational offer for you to make (i.e., can you show that you will be better off at B than at A)?
   b. Should your neighbor accept your offer? Why or why not?
3. Does B represent the optimal combination of beer and pizza you can achieve in the long run, or should you propose a further exchange?
   a. What is the maximum utility level you can reach through exchange from B?
   b. What is the maximum utility level your neighbor can reach through exchange from B?

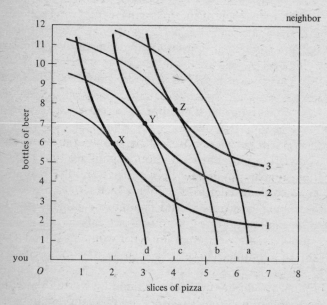

Figure 9. Edgeworth Diagram of Preferences for Pizza and Beer

c. Would these limits be different if you started from point A rather than B? How can you explain this?

d. What factors determine the long-run equilibrium point at which you will settle without further trading? Could this be at five beers and three slices of pizza?

4. What is a *contract curve*?

Draw the contract curve for this problem on the diagram.

a. In what sense is this an equilibrium locus? What are the technical conditions of equilibrium that define points on a contract curve?

b. Since these conditions hold all along the contract curve, why not move to point Z in the long run?

5. The assumptions underlying individual indifference curves must also be accepted in applying an Edgeworth box to the analysis of exchange conditions. Explain briefly how each of the following would affect the diagram.

a. Your neighbor, who is allergic to fish, discovers that the pizza has anchovies on it.

b. You discover that a nearby all-night grocery sells beer.

c. You discover a $20 bill in your coat pocket that you had forgotten about.

6. Suppose that beer and pizza are strictly complementary goods for you; you know from experience that you can eat a maximum of five slices of pizza and that you need one bottle of beer to drink with each slice.

a. Show how this would change the Edgeworth diagram and the resulting contract curve.

b. Given this new diagram, what would be the effect on the contract curve of a change in your neighbor's tastes in favor of beer?

7. What would be the effect on the Edgeworth diagram of indifference curves that are *concave* to the origin

a. For you alone?

b. For both you and your neighbor?

NOTES

1. See, for example, E. Mansfield, *Microeconomic Theory* (New York: Norton, 1970), pp. 44–48.

PART II.
Costs and market supply

15. An all-volunteer armed force (can it work? is it equitable?)

The report of the President's Commission on an All-Volunteer Armed Force, released February 21, 1970, contained the following comments and recommendations:

1. *A return to an all-volunteer force will strengthen our freedoms, remove an inequity now imposed on the expression of patriotism that has never been lacking among our youth, promote the efficiency of the armed forces, and enhance their dignity.*
2. *Reasonable improvements in pay and benefits in the early years of service should increase the number of volunteers by [the required] amounts.*
3. *Although the budgetary expense of a volunteer armed force will be higher than for the present mixed force of volunteers and conscripts, the actual cost will be lower. This seemingly paradoxical statement is true because many of the costs of manning our armed forces today are hidden and are not reflected in the [defense] budget.*

4. . . .*The Commission recommends . . .* [*raising*] *the average level of basic pay from $180 a month to $315 a month. This involves an increase in total compensation (including the value of food, clothing, lodging, and fringe benefits) from $301 a month to $437 a month.* [1]

1. Draw the supply and demand curves for the military manpower market
   a. Under the current draft system.
   b. Under the all-volunteer proposal.
2. Using the relevant analytical concept(s), rewrite statement 2 as an economist might have stated it. [2]
3. What are the costs to the *government* (budgetary costs) of one man-year of military service under each system? What are the opportunity costs to *society* (social costs) of one man-year of service under each system?
4. Think about the answer you have given for question 3 above and use it to explain why the Pentagon tends to "overinvest" in manpower.
   If the all-volunteer proposal were adopted, would you expect to see the Pentagon spend more or less on defense hardware such as ABM's? Why?

Up to this point you have been examining the *efficiency* of the draft as a means of staffing the armed forces, but clearly a major reason for using a draft system is the belief that it is more *equitable* than other, more selective recruiting systems. The next few questions ask you to analyze some equity characteristics of the draft versus an all-volunteer army.

5. Some economists view the draft as imposing a tax (paid in labor services) on the draftee.
   a. Assuming that basic service pay is $2,160 per year, calculate the implicit draftee tax on [3]
      1. A schoolteacher formerly earning $8,000 per year.
      2. A physician formerly earning $40,000 per year.
      3. An unemployed laborer on welfare.

    b. Would this tax be progressive or regressive in its effect?[4]

    c. Can you see an *economic* argument for maintaining that those eligible for the draft should be eligible to vote?

    d. Can this tax be defended by either the *ability-to-pay* or the *benefits-received* principle?

6. If the armed forces became a volunteer organization (but did not have to accept everyone who volunteered), what, if anything, do you anticipate might happen to the composition of military personnel by race, skill level, and social and economic background?[5]

7. Drawing on your results in questions 5 and 6, how would you define *equity* in the staffing of the armed forces?
Do you think the draft lottery is more or less equitable than an all-volunteer system?

8. If we draft men to supply the public good called defense, why not draft them to supply the public goods called postal service and police protection?

9. During the War Between the States, draftees were permitted to hire substitutes to serve for them. Do you think this practice should be revived? Discuss the arguments that could be made both for and against this practice on the grounds of efficiency as well as equity.

NOTES

1. *New York Times*, February 22, 1970. See also A. C. Fisher, "The Cost of Ending the Draft," *AER 59*, 2 (June, 1969): 239–254; W. Y. Oi, "The Economics of Conscription," *SEJ 27*, 2 (October, 1960): 111–117; J. C. Miller III, ed., *Why the Draft?* (Baltimore: Penguin, 1968), esp. pp. 53–90; and W. L. Hansen and B. A. Weisbrod, "Economics of the Military Draft," *QJE 81*, 3 (August, 1967): 395–421.

2. S. H. Altman and R. J. Barro, "Officer Supply—The Impact of Pay, the Draft, and the Vietnam War," *AER 61*, 4 (September, 1971): 649–664.

3. S. H. Altman, "Earnings, Unemployment, and the Supply of

Enlisted Volunteers," *Journal of Human Resources* 4 (Winter, 1969): 38–59.

4. J. R. Davis and N. A. Palomba, "On the Shifting of the Military Draft as a Progressive Tax-in-Kind," *WEJ* 6, 3 (March, 1968): 150–153.

5. M. Janowitz, "Toward an All-Volunteer Military," *The Public Interest*, 27 (Spring, 1972): 104–117. For a different approach to analysis of the Draft, see chap. 41 of this book. See also B. A. Franklin, "Lag in Volunteer Force Spurs Talk of New Draft," *New York Times*, July 1, 1973, p. 1.

16. Airline prices and the effect of technological progress

American airlines are subject to regulation by the Civil Aeronautics Board (CAB) both in the setting of fares and in the scheduling of routes and service. Fares for regularly scheduled flights are set to break even (cover total costs) at 50 percent of capacity on the theory that a scheduled service is supposed to offer readily available flights to the public. According to this philosophy, an airline whose flights were all at 100 percent capacity would not be serving the public adequately. This policy means that relatively high fares for half of the passengers "produce" the flight service for the other half. Willis Player, vice president of Pan Am World Airways, has written:

> It is half-emptiness of the scheduled flights that nurtured
> charter flights. For a charter flight can wait until it is full; or
> it can go only where there are full loads wanting to go; whereas
> a scheduled flight must go, full or empty, when it has said it
> will go, day in and day out, and to destinations that are
> unpopular as well as to destinations that are popular.[1]

1. Suppose that the following hypothetical costs apply to a
   single flight from New York to Los Angeles on a Boeing
   707 with 180 seats.

Maintenance and depreciation	$1200
Fuel	2600
Salary for crew	3600
Administrative salaries of airline officers	2100
Cost of sales and publicity	1100
Office rent	2800
Interest on debt	3550

   a. What are the total fixed costs of the flight?
      What are the total variable costs of the flight?
   b. Under the pricing policy described earlier, what will
      be the regular fare per person on the New York–Los
      Angeles route? (Assume that the CAB holds the air-
      line to a "normal" or competitive profit level.)
   c. What, then, is the marginal cost to the airline of car-
      rying the ninety-first passenger on the flight?
2. Should the airline agree to supply a charter flight for a
   group that offers to guarantee the sale of 140 tickets at a
   maximum price of $60 per seat? Explain your reasoning.
   Assume that the charter would use the same equipment
   with the same costs of operation as the scheduled
   service.
3. Now the airline buys a new, wide-bodied Boeing 747
   that holds 400 passengers and operates with essentially
   the same costs as the 707.
   a. If it continues to follow the same pricing policy, by
      how much will the adoption of the larger-capacity
      plane reduce the New York–Los Angeles fare for the
      traveler on a regularly scheduled flight?
   b. The 747 can make a scheduled flight (without loss)
      with how many empty seats? Compare this to the
      capacity of a completely filled 707 charter flight.
4. This leaves the company in something of a dilemma:
   Should it fly the 747 at half its capacity plus a 707 charter

flight or fly only the 747 with 200 seats sold at the regularly scheduled fares and the 140 charter seats at the $60 charter fare?

Compare these two alternatives on the basis of

a. Total number of passengers carried.

b. Total expenditures by passengers.

c. Total profit to the airline.

5. Can you see any objections that might be raised to adopting the second alternative—that is, charging two different fares for travel on the same plane? Would the two kinds of seats have to be physically differentiated?

NOTES

1. W. Player, "Fill Scheduled Flights with Charters," *New York Times*, July 16, 1972, p. F14.

17. Food for thought— competition versus monopoly

Suppose that you have just been hired by the university's department of housing and dining to operate its food service. You are given a perfectly free hand to set price, determine output (considered as a single product—meals), etc., with the single requirement that you are to maximize profits (or minimize losses). The university accountant is able to provide only the information in the table (page 57) about the results of past operations.

From these meager data you must derive the rest of the information you need to operate intelligently.

1. Fill in the rest of the table.
2. You are now able to determine the best output, _____ meals, which you will sell at a price of _____ each, yielding a total profit of _____.
3. Nevertheless, after a few weeks the president is anxious to know whether you really are maximizing the profits he's been counting on to balance his budget. He asks you to prove with a series of graphs that the P-Q point

Q Meals Sold per Day	P Per Meal	TFC	TVC	TR	MR	TC	MC	AFC	AVC	ATC	Profit
0	$3.50	150	0								
100	3.25	150	300								
200	3.00	150	500								
300	2.75	150	650								
400	2.50	150	750								
500	2.25	150	830								
600	2.00	150	905								
700	1.75	150	995								
800	1.50	150	1110								
900	1.25	150	1260								
1000	1.00	150	1460								

you have chosen represents the very best that can be done with the food service operation.

So you draw up the graphs shown in Figure 10, making sure that they are accurately lined up vertically and completely labeled.

4. And you write a brief statement explaining
   a The profit-maximizing rule you have used.
   b. Why it works.
5. You have succeeded in convincing the president, but now you find that the students plan to boycott your meal service as a result of the P-Q point you have selected according to the profit-maximization rule.
   a. Explain in technical terms what they are trying to do to their demand curve for university meals.
   b. On changes in what parameter(s) does the success of this action depend?
6. Suppose that they succeed so well that your monopolistic position is entirely destroyed and you find yourself in a perfectly competitive situation in which the going rate for meals is now $1.50. What do you do? [Hint: You will have to make some recalculations from the original table. Show the results in Figure 10(f).]

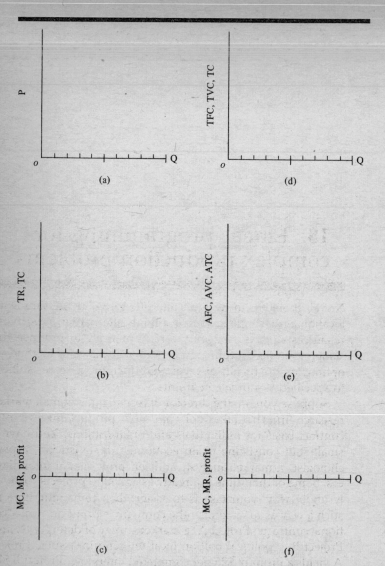

Figure 10. Diagrams for Report to University President

18. Linear programming for complex production problems

Not all problems in resource allocation involve the simple allocation of a single resource among alternative uses; most resources can be used in a variety of ways to produce the same or similar outputs. *Linear programming* is a method of optimizing the results of several production processes subject to specified resource constraints.

Suppose you are the director of research for a small market research firm that takes polls and does product surveys on a contract basis for individuals and organizations. You have a small staff consisting of an economist, a statistician, a psychologist, a market analyst, and ten professional interviewers. Some of their time is already assigned to projects currently under way; your task is to assign their remaining time in such a way as to maximize the company's profit on two additional contracts: Project A, a market survey of detergents, and Project B, a political poll on local referendum issues. Project A yields a profit of $25 per completed interview, Project B $20 per completed interview. Each project can be performed by three different teams made up from the personnel available.

Team 1: the economist, the statistician, the market ana-
         lyst, and nine interviewers. Together the team
         has 400 man-hours to devote to either project
         during the next week. If they spend it all on A,
         they can complete 80 inerviews; on B, they can
         complete 200 interviews—or their time can be di-
         vided proportionately between the two projects.

Team 2: the statistician and three interviewers. This team
         has 110 man-hours available during the next week
         and can complete 110 interviews of either type,
         A or B.

Team 3: your full staff plus 36 extra interviewers hired
         just for the week. Collectively these 50 people
         would have 1800 man-hours available and could
         complete 200 detergent interviews or 90 political
         interviews (or some proportional combination if
         their time is divided between the two projects).

Determine the optimal number of interviews of each type that
should be completed during the next week and the best team
that should be assembled for the job by answering the following questions:

1. Write down the three equations for the resource constraints and the two nonnegativity conditions.
2. Graph these constraints on coordinates, showing the
   number of completed detergent interviews (A) on the
   vertical axis and the number of completed political interviews (B) on the horizontal axis.
   a. On this graph mark the feasible solution space with
      shading.
   b. Is this a convex set? How can you tell? Explain why
      a convex set is necessary to arrive at a solution to this
      problem.
3. Write the equation for the objective function. Diagram
   the objective function on your graph.

4. Give the solution to this problem by specifying
    a. The optimal number of completed interviews of both types that should be produced in the next week.
    b. The best team you should assemble for the job.
    c. How can you prove that the solution you've specified in question 4a is optimal?
  *d. How would you go about solving this problem using the simplex method?
5. On what assumptions does your solution depend (i.e., what are the necessary assumptions of any linear-programming problem)?
6. What is the *dual* of this problem? (State the dual—you don't have to solve it.)

NOTES

1. An excellent description of the geometry and mathematics of linear programming is provided in M. Spencer and L. Seigleman, *Managerial Economics*, rev. ed. (Homewood, Ill.: Irwin, 1964), chap. 15 and in C. E. Ferguson, *Microeconomic Theory*, rev. ed., (Homewood, Ill.: Irwin, 1969), chap. 12.

PART III.
Market structure

A. Monopoly/Monopsony

19. Balfour and the Greek monopoly

For years the Balfour company has had a virtual monopoly over the manufacture of "official" jewelry for fraternities and sororities. It prevents the entry of competitors by persuading the national headquarters of the "Greek" societies to grant it exclusive rights to the use of their official insignia.

1. Draw a diagram representing Balfour's market conditions (show both cost and revenue conditions).
2. Why is marginal revenue less than average revenue for the monopolist? Is this also true for the perfectly competitive firm? Why or why not?
3. Use your diagram to define *monopolistic profit*.
   a. In what sense can this be said to represent a misallocation of resources?
   b. Does this amount represent a real welfare loss to society, merely a transfer of consumer's surplus to producers (i.e., no *net* loss), or some of both? Explain with reference to your diagram.

4. Show on the diagram the effects of a policy under which the Greek societies begin to charge Balfour a royalty of $1 per piece per item for each item of official jewelry it sells.

   Is this a desirable policy from the viewpoint of fraternity members? Why or why not?

5. Would it be preferable for the Greeks simply to take competitive bids for the use of their insignia once a year? (Show on your diagram the quantity and price you would expect Balfour to bid in competition.)

20. The Brasserie (or, what price onion soup?)

A popular French restaurant in New York City, the Brasserie, is open 24 hours a day, seven days a week. One of its specialties—onion soup—appears on the lunch-dinner menu (served from 11:00 A.M. to 10:00 P.M.) at a price of 95c and on the after-theater menu (served from 10:00 P.M. to 5:00 A.M.) at a price of $1.10.

1. Is this a case of true price discrimination? By what criterion is this determined?
2. What two conditions are necessary for *successful* price discrimination? Show how this case does or does not conform to these two conditions.
3. Is this, then, a rational pricing policy for the Brasserie to use (show why charging different prices will or will not maximize its profits).
4. Can it be said that after-theater customers are "cheated" by this procedure? Why or why not? Using utility terms, explain how you would define being "cheated."

21. What price economics?

Suppose that there are two sections of your economics course taught by the same professor—one at 8:00 A.M. and the other at 10:00 A.M. In order to equalize class sizes, the university decides to charge a higher tuition rate for the 10:00 section.

1. Is this a true case of price discrimination?
2. If so, show how it conforms to the requirements for successful price discrimination. If not, explain how it fails to fulfill the necessary conditions for price discrimination.
3. Are students in the 10:00 section cheated by this process? Define and use the concept of consumer's surplus to answer this.
4. If the university decides to use this pricing policy for all of its classes, how should it determine how many classes to offer at each hour? Give the allocation rule and explain it in common-sense terms.
5. Suppose that instead of setting a fixed tuition rate per credit hour the university registrar haggles with each

student for the maximum price he is willing to pay. Would this result in price discrimination? Would it be "unfair" to students? Explain.

What *advantages* might accrue from such a price-by-bargaining process to the university? to the student?

22. Our ailing medical system[1]

Discontent with the pricing and allocation of medical services in the United States has reached major proportions in the past few years. Despite some spectacular advances in specialized technology (such as heart transplants) in the provision of ordinary care to the average citizen the United States has slipped badly—to twentieth place among the industrialized nations of the world in infant mortality and to eighteenth place in male survival rates. For this dubious record we pay the largest percentage (8 percent) of our national GNP for medical care and have recently experienced inflation of medical costs at more than twice the average inflation rate; yet the United States is the only major industrial nation without some form of national health insurance. The Kennedy-Griffiths bill calling for a prepaid national health insurance plan is currently before the U.S. Senate.

As one writer has put it, ". . . health care in this country is wastefully organized, unjustly distributed, and remarkably ineffective." The reasons for this situation include monopoly power, discriminatory pricing, and most recently, ill-designed government programs like Medicare. To find out how the market system that provides us so efficiently with neckties and thumbtacks can work so unsatisfactorily in providing essential medical services, consider the following questions. They are divided into two sections: first, an analysis of the position of the individual doctor in the U.S. medical system, and second, an examination of the "system" by which medical services are delivered.

I. One conspicuous feature of medical practice in the United States, stoutly defended by the American Medical Association (AMA), is first-degree price discrimination by the individual physician. Called *fee-for-service pricing*, it permits each doctor to charge different prices to different patients for the same service—in short, the doctor charges what the market will bear in each case.

1. Explain briefly how the market for physicians' services conforms to the necessary conditions for successful first-degree price discrimination.[2]
Why doesn't a doctor who discriminates in pricing lose his richer patients to other doctors—say, young doctors just building up their practices?

2. What effect, if any, do you think discriminatory pricing has on the geographic distribution of doctors between urban and rural areas?[3] Explain.

3. What justification can there be for permitting price discrimination in medical services? Is it any different from permitting discrimination in electric utility rates?

4. Do you think this is a desirable method of redistributing income? Why or why not?
What evidence is there that the resulting income distribution is in the "right" direction (i.e., from the rich to the poor)?

5. In a recent empirical study[4] it was found that doctors have a backward-bending supply-of-labor curve of the form $S = 30-2P$. The following important elasticities

were also estimated: price elasticity of demand for physician services = −.96; price elasticity of supply of physician services = −.91; elasticity of price (fees) with respect to insurance coverage = +.36.

a. Draw the specified supply curve on Figure 11. Explain the meaning of the supply elasticity figure (−.91).

b. Is it true, as the AMA has argued, that any program or legislation that reduces or sets an upper limit to the fees doctors can charge will reduce the supply of physicians' services?

c. Is it correct in this market situation to say that there is a doctor *shortage*?[5]

d. What would be the effect on this shortage of the Kennedy-Griffiths bill, which calls for a reduction of the average fee charged by physicians below F_1? Would it be better to increase the fee to F_3?

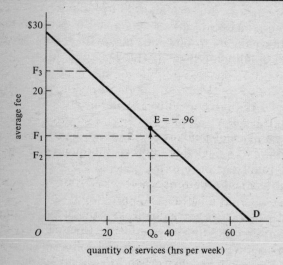

Figure 11. Market for Physicians' Services in the United States

II. In addition to the fees charged by individual doctors, a large and increasing share of the patient's medical bill consists of hospital charges, which have risen even faster than doctors' fees. Taken together, these costs can mean catastrophic financial loss in cases of serious and prolonged treatment. Blue Cross was one of the first and largest group insurance plans designed to spread this risk among all of the members of a community. But Blue Cross (a nonprofit organization) and other commercial insurance companies have been unable or unwilling to control the rising spiral of medical costs.[6]

In 1965, over the strong opposition of the AMA, the federal government entered the field with Medicare, a payment program for people over 65. The AMA argued that Medicare would destroy incentives for doctors, reduce the quantity and quality of care, and destroy the sacred patient-doctor relationship. The actual results of Medicare have been described by government officials as "surprising," "highly disappointing," and even "disastrous." To see why, it is necessary to examine the overall system (or, as some have charged, "nonsystem") of medical-service delivery in the United States.

6. How would you classify the structure of the market for medical services (competitive, monopolistic, oligopolistic, etc.)?
   Why don't doctors and hospitals advertise and compete for patients? Would this improve the quality of care and/or reduce its price to the patient?
   Would you favor the proposal that licensing of doctors be eliminated as a barrier to entry?

7. Medicare provides for federal payment of physicians' "customary fees" for the treatment of people over 65; hospitalization costs above an initial $50 are also covered. It is estimated that Medicare has increased the overall ability to pay of the population by 10 percent. In the period between the introduction of Medicare in 1965

and the freezing of prices for medical services by President Nixon in 1972, average physicians' fees increased at a rate of 6.8 percent per year while the overall inflation rate was about 3.2 percent per year.

a. Explain the meaning of the +.36 elasticity figure given in question 5.

b. How much, if any, of the 6.8 percent increase in physicians' fees during the period can be attributed to the Medicare program? Could this price increase have been predicted?

Does the pricing behavior implied by this elasticity tend to support or undermine the justification for price discrimination advanced in question 3?

c. How would you evaluate the *distributional* effects of Medicare to date (i.e., can it be sensibly argued that Medicare, though inefficient, distributes access to medical care more "fairly")?

8. Testifying against the operation of New York State's Medicaid program (a payment program for the poor regardless of age), one doctor has said: "The state Medicaid program pays only $12 for the consultation of a specialist, while his normal charge is $25. The state has ordered every doctor to treat Medicaid patients, and at fees set by the state. This has got to be a form of involuntary servitude."[8]

a. Is this view consistent with the justification for fee-for-service pricing given in question 3?

b. Do you agree that it is involuntary servitude? Explain your reasoning.

9. One critic of the present system has said: "The present system of medical practice and insurance rewards long and expensive treatment of illness rather than the delivery of health and prevention of disease."

a. How might prepaid group practice reverse these incentives? (Prepaid group practices like the Kaiser Plan in California and HIP in New York consist of a group of doctors, usually with their own hospital facilities, who undertake to provide whatever care is necessary to subscribers for a fixed annual charge.)

10. Do you think the cure for the financial pains of the medical consumer is a rearrangement of the method of payment (prepaid group insurance plans, national health insurance, etc.), government regulation of prices in the medical field (like the regulation of electric utility rates), structural changes in the organization of the medical industry itself, or some combination of these?[9] Explain.

11. When we use the market to allocate medical care, we are really adopting the principle of distribution to the highest bidder. Do you think market allocation is the best process for medical services, or is there a better alternative? (Consider not only the issue of distributional equity but also effects on the total supply of services that would be provided under alternative schemes.) Would you agree or disagree with Baird:

Today's hospitals sell health at an extraordinary price. Since when more resources are devoted to the production of health less are available for the production of other things consumers want, it is time that we drop the fiction that the provision of health is an activity different from the provision of other goods. It is legitimate to insist that a given level of health be attained as cheaply as possible, and the most effective way to bring this about is to abandon the voluntary (non-profit) in favor of the proprietary (profit-making) hospital. Consumers do not need regulation to protect them when competition prevails.[10]

NOTES

1. See "Our Ailing Medical System," *Fortune* (January, 1970): 79 ff. for a more complete discussion of issues raised here.

2. R. A. Kessel, "Price Discrimination in Medicine," *Journal of Law and Economics 1* (October, 1958), reprinted in Mansfield, *Readings,* pp. 252–271.

3. G. V. Rimlinger and H. B. Steele, "An Economic Interpreta-

tion of the Spatial Distribution of Physicians in the United States,"
SEJ 30, 1 (July, 1963): 1–12.

4. M. S. Feldstein, "The Rising Price of Physicians' Services,"
Review of Economics and Statistics 52, 2 (May, 1970): 121–133.

5. R. Fein, *The Doctor Shortage* (Washington, D.C.: Brookings,
1967).

6. J. Ehrenreich, "The Blue Cross We Bear," *Washington Monthly*
(May, 1969).

7. T. Marmor, "Why Medicare Helped Raise Doctors' Fees,"
Trans-action 5, 9 (September, 1968): 14–19.

8. R. D. Lyons, "The Poor Have a Friend in Court," *New York
Times*, April 23, 1972.

9. M. Pauly, *Medical Care at Public Expense: A Study in Applied
Welfare Economics* (New York: Praeger, 1971) and Y. Barzel, "Pro-
ductivity and the Price of Medical Services," *JPE 77*, 6 (November–
December, 1969): 1014–1027. See also M. Pauly and M. Redisch,
"The Not-for-Profit Hospital as a Physicians' Cooperative," *AER
63*, 1 (March, 1973): 87–100.

10. C. W. Baird, "On Profits and Hospitals," *Journal of Economic
Issues 5*, 1 (March, 1971): 57–66.

23. The pricing of textbooks

There are several features of the publishing business that strongly influence pricing decisions for textbooks; the major cost elements are initial expenses of preparation and payment of the author. Substantial fixed costs in the form of expenses for editing, typesetting, proofreading, advertising, and in some cases original research are paid for by the publisher. After the initial expenses have been incurred, the marginal cost of each copy printed includes the costs of labor, paper, printing, binding, selling, and warehousing, all amounting to about one-third of the book's total costs. The author is most commonly paid a royalty calculated as a percentage of the publisher's receipts from each copy sold.[1] The publisher counts on his contract rights to the final book, enforced through copyright law, and his ability to judge the market to recoup these expenses plus a profit. Figure 12 shows the market for a new hard-cover economics textbook as estimated by the publisher.

1. Why does the demand curve slope downward?
   Would this be a correct representation of demand conditions if copyright protection were repealed?
   Why or why not?
   Will this demand curve be a correct representation for the second and third years the book is in print? Explain.

2. Draw in the marginal-cost curve and explain its shape. How will this influence total costs? (Draw in the ATC curve—you will need it for a later question.)

3. The publisher says: "With high initial fixed costs it pays to spread them over as many copies as possible. Hence, our policy is to maximize the number of copies sold."
   a. What is the profit-maximizing price for the publisher to set for this textbook?
   b. How does this compare with the results of his sales-maximization policy stated earlier?

4. Now consider the author who receives a royalty of 15 percent of the price of each copy sold.
   a. What price would the *author* choose in order to maximize his royalties?

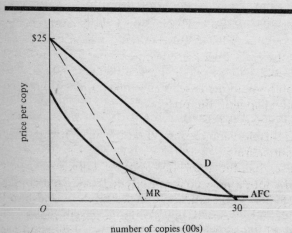

Figure 12. Estimated Market for New Economics Textbook

b. Compare the author's and the publisher's preferred prices. How can you explain the conflict of interest between author and publisher on this matter (i.e., why isn't what's good for the publisher also good for the author)?

c. Would this conflict of interest be eliminated if the publisher gave the author a share of the profits instead of royalties? Explain your reasoning.

d. Under which payment scheme, royalties or profit sharing, would the author be better off? Explain.

5. A common way to advertise a textbook is to give complimentary copies to teachers of related courses. (Recall that the marginal cost of extras is small.) Suppose that the author of the textbook requests that complimentary copies be sent to a list of 20 people he has compiled. The publisher has learned from experience that for every 20 complimentary copies he sends out he receives paid orders for 5 additional copies.

a. Should the publisher send the 20 copies?

b. Can the publisher show that it is in the author's economic interest to withdraw his request for complimentary copies?

6. An alternate means of generating sales might be to make the book itself more attractive—say, by using color for clearer diagrams. The publisher estimates that this would add $4000 to the production costs of the book and would increase sales to 1600 copies from 1300 with no change in the price.

Should he use color?

Would this decision be different if the author were paid by profit sharing?

7. Suppose that the publisher and the bookstores concerned adopt a new policy of buying back used copies of the textbook but refusing to resell them second-hand (i.e., they burn all used copies bought from students).

a. Would you expect the price elasticity of demand for new copies at the publisher's price to increase or decrease as a result of this policy?

b. How can you explain the observation that publishers frequently follow first-run hard-cover editions of their books with paperback editions even though these compete directly with each other? Why do you think most textbooks aren't published as paperbacks from the start?

8. Now suppose that the publisher prints another economics textbook that is competitive with the first one. He estimates the market demand for the second book at exactly half of that for the first (that is, the demand curve for the second book coincides with the marginal revenue curve for the first).

Should the publisher set the price of the second book at the same level or at a lower one than that of the first to maximize his joint profits on sales of both textbooks? (Assume that the costs of publication are the same for both books.)

Prove your answer from the diagram.

9. Would you agree or disagree with this statement:[2] "Copyright laws, like patents, are merely a means for conferring monopoly power over a published work and ought to be abolished."

NOTES

1. Publisher's receipts are net of the bookseller's discount (usually 20 percent) but before deduction of production expenses. See S. Horvitz, "The Pricing of Textbooks and the Remuneration of Authors," *AEA Papers 56*, 2 (May, 1966): 412–420.

2. See R. Hurt, "The Economic Rationale of Copyright," *AEA Papers 56*, 2 (May, 1966): 421–432.

24. Efficient postal service—public or private enterprise?

In 1972, after many years of deficit operation, the U.S. Post Office was finally converted into a quasipublic enterprise, the U.S. Postal Service, and required to at least break even in its overall operations. The purpose of this change was to increase the Post Office's operating efficiency by removing it as a source of political patronage and thereby permitting automation of some services as well as rearrangement of postal rates for the four basic classes of mail: first-class letters, second-class periodicals, third-class miscellaneous printed matter, and fourth-class merchandise.[1] It was hoped that greater efficiency would also speed up average delivery times.

The new Postal Service now faces two interesting sets of questions: (1) What is the correct pricing policy for various classes of mail that will generate revenues equal to or greater than average total cost? (2) Is postal service a true "natural monopoly," or should the government permit private competitors to enter this market? Evidence of the actual costs of various classes of mail service is scarce but suggests that the overall average and marginal costs for a particular post office are as shown in Figure 13.

1. What is the optimum size of the Philadelphia post office?
2. What effect, if any, would you expect automation of certain sorting and canceling functions to have on this optimal size? How would this be reflected in the diagram?

Each class of mail was formerly priced by congressional policy on the basis of value of service (first class), cost of service (second and fourth class), or public-service value (third class). This meant that first-class mail returned a small "profit" over cost that was used to cover deficits on second-, third-, and fourth-class mail; third class includes most of what is commonly called "junk mail."

3. Help the new Postal Service rethink and revise its rate structure by answering the following questions:
   If *only one rate* can be charged for all classes of mail, what should the rate per piece be

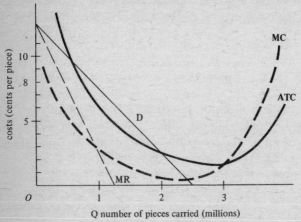

Figure 13. Costs and Revenue for Philadelphia Postal Services, All Classes
(Q = millions of pieces carried)

a. If the Postal Service seeks to maximize profits?

b. If it seeks to maximize the amount of postal services (pieces carried) that can be provided without deficit?

4. Now suppose that Congress votes to permit price discrimination by the Postal Service. To simplify, assume that only two classes of mail are distinguished: A-class letters and periodicals, and B-class merchandise and miscellaneous material.

How should A- and B-class rates be set (i.e., describe how you would go about determining these rates analytically)

a. If the Postal Service is a profit maximizer?

b. If its objective is to maximize service?

c. Could the Postal Service afford to create a class of mail (C-class congressional mail) that would go at a rate less than its marginal cost without creating a postal deficit? If so, how; if not, why not?

d. The following average and marginal costs have been estimated for first- and third-class mail in 1959.[2] Does this evidence support or refute the popular feeling that first-class mail rates subsidize the carrying of unsolicited junk mail (third-class)? Explain.

	ATC per Piece	AR per Piece	MC per Piece
First class	4.20c	4.54c	2.65c
Third class	3.97c	2.54c	3.16c

In December, 1971 a private enterprise, the Intercity Postal Service Association (IPSA), was formed to deliver Christmas mail in 20 major cities for 5c per piece (the regular first-class rate was 8c). A federal court ruled IPSA illegal on the ground that it violated federal law prohibiting private enterprises from carrying first-class mail or delivering through mailboxes or letter slots. This restriction of entry has been defended by arguing that postal service is a *natural monopoly* and as such ought to be reserved to the government.

Not to be deterred by this argument, in June, 1972 Thomas M. Murray, president of the Independent Postal System of

America, announced that his organization had opened offices in more than 100 U.S. cities, including Philadelphia, and would deliver mail in plastic bags hung from doorknobs. The organization would "employ postmasters on a franchise basis, map out routes with computers, and then sell about 3000 routes for $1000 each."[3]

5. Define in analytical terms the necessary conditions for a natural monopoly.
   By your definition is postal service a natural monopoly?
6. Do natural monopolies necessarily have to be owned and operated by the government?[4] Why or why not?
7. Do you think Mr. Murray's Independent Postal System should be permitted to compete with the new U.S. Postal Service or not? Explain your reasoning.

NOTES

1. R. J. Willey, "Taking the Post Office Out of Politics," *The Public Interest*, 15 (Spring, 1969): 57–71. For the view of one of these political appointees, see L. O'Brien, "Crisis Coming in the Mails," *U.S. News and World Report* (April 24, 1967): 58–62.

2. M. S. Baratz, "Cost Behavior and Pricing Policy in the Post Office," *Land Economics 38*, 4 (November, 1962): 312.

3. See "Philadelphia Area to Get Competition in Postal Services," *New York Times*, June 11, 1972.

4. See M. Friedman, *op. cit.*, p. 29.

4. One possible reaction to monopsony is the formation of a countervailing monopoly power through unionization.

   a. Would it be to the advantage of teachers in this situation to unionize? Why or why not?

   b. If the union wants to maximize the number of teachers employed, what salary should it bargain for?

5. Recently a trend has developed toward decentralization of large metropolitan school systems into a number of autonomous districts, each of which hires and fires its own teachers. What effect would you expect decentralization to have on:

   a. Teachers' salary levels.

   b. The general level of school taxes.

6. How would you respond to a board of education member who offered this opinion: "This is not really a problem of the monopsony power of the board of education but one of labor force immobility."

7. What other factors besides monopsony power might contribute to the determination of salary levels for a given school district?

   What noneconomic reasons might make decentralization attractive to local voters despite its economic costs?

NOTES

1. J. H. Landon and R. N. Baird, "Monopsony in the Market for Public School Teachers," *AER 61*, 5 (December, 1971): 966–971. See also W. C. Neale, "The Peculiar Economics of Professional Sports," *QJE 78*, 1 (February, 1964): 1–14.

26. AT&T—a case of regulated monopoly

In virtually every country of the world, telephone service is provided by a monopoly, sometimes "private" and sometimes state-owned, reflecting substantial economies of scale and a technology that would make the provision of competitive service through duplication of facilities extremely costly. In the United States, American Telephone & Telegraph (AT&T) is a natural monopoly regulated as a public utility by the public-utilities commission of each state.[1]

1. Figure 15 shows the market for telephone service in the United States assume that all calls are local).[2]
   a. What justification is there for drawing marginal cost as the horizontal line ATC?
   b. What is the profit-maximizing price for AT&T to charge if it is unregulated? (Recall that AT&T has private stockholders who want as high a rate of return on their investment as the management can earn.)
   c. Show on the diagram the monopolistic profit the company will earn at this price.
   d. How can you explain the fact that AT&T spends considerable sums for advertising, even though as a mo-

nopoly it is already guaranteed the whole market? Is this expenditure contrary to the stockholders' interest?

2. Suppose that you are appointed as a public representative to the public-utilities commission to represent the interests of the *consumer* of telephone services.

   a. What reasons are there for you, a public representative, to view the profit-maximizing price as unsatisfactory?

   b. If the purpose of a public utility is to serve the greatest number of people without a deficit, what price and quantity should the regulatory commission set for telephone service?

3. The courts have held that public utilities are entitled to earn a "fair rate of return" on the invested capital of their stockholders.

   a. How, if at all, would the diagram need to be changed to reflect this fair rate of return?

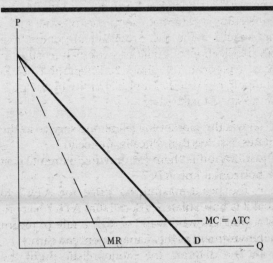

Figure 15. Market for Local Telephone Service
(Q = Number of Calls)

b. How is a fair rate of return defined?

4. The public-utilities commission has the following regulatory instruments to use: (a) price ceiling and (b) excise tax.

   a. Show on the diagram the effect of imposing a 10 percent excise tax on all telephone calls. What determines how much of this tax will be passed on to the consumer in the form of higher prices?

   b. Which of these two devices, price control or excise taxes, do you think is the better regulatory tool? Why?

*5. One objection to monopoly is that it misallocates resources by charging a higher price and producing a smaller quantity of services than would emerge under competitive pricing, thereby imposing a welfare loss on society. Analyze the welfare loss imposed on telephone subscribers in the following steps, using your diagram.

   a. What would be the competitive price and quantity of service supplied in the absence of monopoly?

   b. Specify on the diagram
      1) The amount of "excess profit" received by AT&T.
      2) The total resources required to expand output to its competitive level (= producer's surplus).
      3) The net loss of welfare (= producer's surplus − consumer's surplus).[3]

   c. The welfare loss you have just identified is a static effect. Can you think of any *dynamic* effects of monopoly that may be undesirable? desirable?

6. Cable television, a new development in communications technology, can provide two-way communication service with visual as well as audio dimensions to every household now receiving telephone service.

   a. Do you think cable systems should be publicly or privately owned? On what considerations does this depend?

   b. Should AT&T be permitted to own cable systems?[4]

NOTES

1. There are a number of small, independent, local telephone companies in the United States, but these are linked to the Bell system and price their services in accordance with Bell rates. For a history of the part played by these companies in product and service innovation, see J. Goulden, *Monopoly* (New York: Pocket Books, 1970).

2. Some of the more complex problems of differentiating the price structure are discussed in S. C. Littlechild, "Peak-Load Pricing of Telephone Calls," *The Bell Journal of Economics and Management Science 1*, 2 (Autumn, 1970): 191–210.

3. See A. Harberger, "Monopoly and Resource Allocation," *AER 44*, 2 (May, 1954) and D. Schwartzman, "The Effect of Monopoly on Price," *JPE 67*, 4 (1959). Both of these studies estimate the welfare loss from monopoly in the United States to be small.

4. See J. Goulden, *op. cit.*, chap. 6 for a description of the battle between AT&T and President Kennedy over control of the Comsat satellite system.

B. Oligopoly

27. The pricing of steel—oligopoly in action

In January, 1971 Bethlehem Steel announced an average price increase of 12 percent on major steel items (primarily plates and structural shapes). The Nixon administration, in a reaction reminiscent of President Kennedy's in 1962,[1] labeled these new prices inflationary and brought "jawboning" pressures to bear on the rest of the steel companies not to follow suit by threatening to reduce tariffs on cheaper Japanese steel imports. Nevertheless, a spokesman for one of the other firms said ". . . the companies absolutely must stand by these Bethlehem increases, which are absolutely necessary [to cover higher costs]."[2]

1. Does jawboning make any economic sense? That is, if its price increases are *not* truly justified by cost increases, won't Bethlehem simply be pricing itself out of the market anyway?
2. Draw a diagram for the steel market as United States Steel (one firm) might view it, and use your diagram to explain the effects Nixon is trying to achieve through

jawboning. Why were these pressures applied to U.S. Steel and other firms instead of directly to Bethlehem itself?

3. Now draw a diagram showing the market for the whole steel industry. (Assume that the industry is composed of only two firms, Bethlehem and U.S. Steel.)

Use this diagram to explain one possible way in which the new price of steel may have been determined.

4. U.S. steel companies have been extremely slow to adopt the more advanced continuous-casting process developed by the Austrians and the Japanese after World War II, even though it reduces costs per ton by about 50 percent.[3] Moreover, until this recent price increase the steel industry had an unwritten rule (initiated by Bethlehem itself) of making only one price change in any twelve-month period.

Use your knowledge of oligopolistic industry structures to explain

a. Why the U.S. steel industry has been technologically backward.[4]

What would Galbraith have to say about this in view of his *New Industrial State* thesis?

b. Why steel prices to the consumer have been relatively "rigid" (what some critics have called "a generally insensitive, utility-like price policy by domestic producers").

NOTES

1. For a discussion of the Kennedy action, see E. Mansfield, *Monopoly Power and Economic Performance* (New York: Norton, 1968), pp. 97–104.

2. *New York Times*, January 17, 1971, p. F2.

3. Austrian and Japanese mills began installing continuous-casting processes in 1952. The U.S. mills didn't follow suit until 1962, after imports of Japanese steel had made serious inroads into the American market.

4. W. Adams and J. B. Dirlam, "Steel Imports and Vertical Oli-

gopoly Power," *AER 54*, 4 (September, 1964): 626–655 and comments by R. E. Slesinger, G. A. Hone and D. S. Schoenbrod, and Adams and Dirlam in *AER 56*, 1 (March, 1966): 152–168.

28. General Motors meets the Price Board

The Nixon administration's system of price and wage controls introduced in the fall of 1971 essentially turned *every* industry into a regulated one. In this problem you are asked to examine the pricing policies of General Motors (GM), a member of the oligopolistic automobile industry, before and after the introduction of price controls. Imagine that you are the staff economist for the Price Board and are using Figure 16 to analyze the effects of various Board actions on automobile prices.

1. Why is the demand curve broken ("kinked")? Explain briefly the relationship of marginal revenue to average revenue for GM.
2. How (if at all) will the diagram for the industry as a whole differ from that for GM?
3. Show on the diagram the equilibrium price, quantity, and profit for GM *before* price regulation. What determines P^*?

4. What effect would you expect on the price of GM automobiles if the Price Board imposed a reduction in the price of steel on the steel industry?
5. Suppose now that the Price Board sets a price ceiling for GM that cuts its unregulated price by one-third.
   Draw the new price ceiling on the diagram and show its effects on *quantity* and *profit* for the firm.
   Will this be a favorable policy from the *consumer's* standpoint? (Consider long-term as well as short-term effects, and remember that consumers are also workers.)
6. What is the minimum price the Board could set for GM without imposing a loss on the company?
   Would you favor setting this minimum as the official price ceiling? Why or why not?
7. In his *New Industrial State* Galbraith argues that oligopolistic industry structures in the U.S. may be *dynamically* efficient in promoting rapid technological progress by devoting large portions of their profits to research and development of new products.

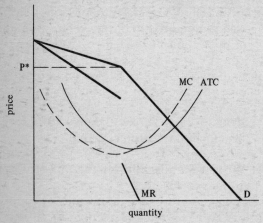

Figure 16. Market for General Motors Automobiles as Perceived by General Motors

    a. Do you think the U.S. automobile industry has been dynamically efficient, even though it has been statically inefficient? Explain your reasoning.

    b. What effect do you think the elimination of all tariffs on foreign-made automobiles would have on the *static* efficiency of the U.S. auto industry? on its *dynamic* efficiency?

8. How would you evaluate this statement if made by an industry spokesman appearing before the Price Board:

Any action taken by this Board which depresses the price of automobiles below the current market price [i.e., P* in the diagram] will seriously retard the ability of our industry to develop an electric car capable of reducing the environmental effects of mass private automobile travel.

29. Game theory and racial discrimination in housing

The decision problem known in game theory as the Prisoner's Dilemma is a two-person, nonzero-sum "game" in which no collaboration is permitted between participants before or during the decision process. Each participant is asked to decide on a strategy or action independently of the other, although the resulting payoffs of each strategy are interdependent. In such situations it emerges that "rational" independent decisions may vary significantly from the optimal decision that would be made if the participants were to collaborate. The Prisoner's Dilemma situation has been used to analyze the pattern of decisions to sell or not sell by white homeowners in suburban residential areas opened to racial minorities by civil-rights legislation.[1]

Suppose that Mr. White and Mr. Green own $22,000 homes in a neighborhood into which Mr. Black, a member of a minority group, has just moved. White, who is personally prejudiced against Black, wants to sell his house and move out, but Green, a civil libertarian, points out that White and others like him who let their prejudices rule them in this matter will simply succeed in imposing a loss on everyone in the neighborhood, sellers and nonsellers alike, by driving down property values. Green is not a prejudiced man and would not voluntarily move, but he cannot afford a large drop in the value of his property since he has secured a loan to finance his son's college education with a $16,000 mortgage on his house. Feeling that he cannot discuss this matter with White without appearing to conspire with the prejudiced group, Green consults the city tax assesor for facts on which to base his own individual decision. He is told that under similar situations in other neighborhoods if both houses (White's and Green's) are put on the market, their value can be expected to drop about $4,000 per property; if only one sells, his house will bring about $20,000 but the remaining unsold properties will fall in value to about $15,000.

1. Construct a payoff table for White and Green in which each has two possible alternatives: to sell or not sell.
2. What is the optimal decision for Green to make *individually* (without consultation with White)? Explain.
   Suppose now that Green announces his decision to White. What is White's optimal strategy?
3. How does the result of this strategy compare, for Green, with the outcome of the best possible *overall* strategy?
   a. Would you advise Green in these circumstances to overcome his scruples and form a coalition with White? Why or why not?
      If such a coalition were formed, what would be the optimal strategy for both White and Green to adopt?
   b. It is sometimes said that this collaborative decision strategy is unstable. What does this mean?
4. If we assume that White and Green determine their strategies (individual or collaborative) on the basis of the *utility* (or disutility) of various payoffs, what effects other than the dollar amounts you've used in the table

do you think might be taken into consideration by the two men?

5. Looking at the payoff table, what condition would be necessary to reverse Green's optimal individual strategy?

   What policies can you think of to bring about this condition?

6. Do you think this game theory analysis provides a convincing explanation for the observed pattern of racial integration in housing known as the "tipping point" phenomenon—that is, the observation that whole neighborhoods switch suddenly from white to black ownership or vice versa after the first moves toward integration?

   Would a quota system for both blacks and whites be an effective way of maintaining a truly integrated neighborhood?[2]

NOTES

1. Applications have been made by Smolensky *et al.* to the rental market in the following: E. Smolensky, *The Economics of Antipoverty Programs Involving Income-in-Kind, Phase I.: The Public Housing Case* (Chicago: Chicago University Center for Urban Studies, 1967), Appendix C; E. Smolensky, S. Becker, and H. Mollotch, *The Prisoner's Dilemma and Ghetto Expansion* (Ljubljana: American-Yugoslav Project in Urban and Regional Planning Studies, 1967); O. A. Davis and A. B. Winston, "Economics of Urban Renewal," *Law and Contemporary Problems 26,* 1 (Winter, 1961); a more complete treatment can be found in A. Rapoport, *Prisoner's Dilemma* (Ann Arbor: University of Michigan Press, 1965).

2. Such a quota scheme is reported to have been adopted by the town of Shaker Heights, Ohio in an attempt to maintain an effectively integrated community.

30. *The Encounter*, a drama in five lines

John Kenneth Galbraith meets Ralph Nader coming out of a Senate hearing in which he (Nader) has just made a convincing argument in favor of tighter government regulation of weight and packaging standards for food products (call it a "truth-in-packaging" bill).

GALBRAITH: Ralph, you're a smart young lawyer, but you're wasting your time and talents trying to preserve an obsolete myth.

NADER: You're wrong, J. K., the consumer is alive and well in Washington, D.C.

Drawing on your knowledge of Galbraith's views, the perfectly competitive model, and microeconomic theory in general, analyze this dialogue by discussing the following points.

1. What is the "obsolete myth" Galbraith refers to, and why does he argue that it is obsolete?

2. Give your own reasons for agreeing or disagreeing with him on this point.

3. Do you think Galbraith's image of the modern corporation is essentially the same as the oligopolistic firm in microtheory? Why or why not?

4. Milton Friedman is generally regarded as a "conservative" economist and Galbraith as a "liberal" one. Yet Friedman is the one who first proposed the negative income tax, and Galbraith appears to be arguing for big business and the benefits of oligopoly. How would you explain this apparent confusion to an average citizen who had not read works by either of these authors?

31. The international airline cartel

The International Air Transport Association (IATA) is a cartel of 108 European and American airlines flying transatlantic routes. Most European members are government-supported airlines; U.S. member airlines are regulated by the Civil Aeronautics Board but are independent profit-making firms. The IATA serves as a forum for the exchange of technical information and the maintenance of safety standards, but its primary function is price fixing—it sets and enforces uniform prices for all flights of the same class on each transatlantic route. Since some airlines operate with higher costs than others, the uniform price must be set to yield an acceptable revenue even to the most inefficient airline. Price schedules are revised periodically as necessary.

1. How can you explain the fact that the U.S. government holds cartels to be illegal inside the United States yet permits its federally regulated airlines to join an international cartel?
   What is wrong with cartels as a form of industrial organization within the United States?

2. How can the IATA determine the uniform price that
   will maximize the collective profits of all 108 member
   airlines taken together?
3. Once the uniform price has been set, how will the total
   amount of traffic (number of flights on each route) be
   portioned out among the member airlines?
   Under this scheme will the U.S. airlines get more or less
   than their competitive share of the transatlantic travel
   business?
4. What sanctions does the IATA have to enforce its uniform price schedules?

In the spring of 1971 *Time* magazine reported:

> *An Anglo-North American coalition of Pan Am, TWA, Air
> Canada and Britain's BOAC is pressing for broadly lower fares
> to woo more passengers. The U.S. Civil Aeronautics Board
> also supports this position. But an orthodox faction—including
> Air France, Swissair, Germany's Lufthansa, The Netherlands'
> KLM, and some carriers from developing countries—fears
> that widespread reductions would simply produce smaller
> profits and no substantial increase in business.* [1]

5. Suppose that you know that the price elasticity of demand for transatlantic travel is 2.2. What can you tell
   the IATA about this price controversy?
   Is there some other reason why the "orthodox faction"
   might rationally resist a general reduction in fares?
6. Having failed to achieve the desired reduction in fares,
   in the summer of 1971 a number of airlines instituted
   "youth fares" for travel to Europe at about half the regular economy class rate. Legal suits were filed almost
   immediately against the participating airlines charging
   "age discrimination"; as one spokesman put it, "Why
   should youth travel be subsidized by everyone else?"
   a. If you were legal counsel for the defendant airlines,

what arguments might you make in defense of the youth fares?

b. If you were the judge in this case, how would you rule and why?

NOTES

1. "Exodus 1971: New Bargains in the Sky," *Time* (July 19, 1971): 52–57. See also P. J. C. Friedlander, "The Politics of Youth Fares," *New York Times*, April 23, 1972.

32. Monopolistic competition in the fashion industry

Monopolistic competition is a mixed form of market structure in which there are many producers and entry is easy, but products are differentiated, giving each producer some control over his segment of the market. Consider the fashion industry. The same general product—say, women's dresses—is highly differentiated by style to meet a wide variety of tastes. Entry into the production process is easy—the only capital needed is a pair of scissors, a sewing machine, and a three-month lease on a Seventh Avenue loft. Every season many small companies enter and leave the market, their fate depending heavily on their ability to prejudge the changing tastes of consumers. (Only the very largest couturier establishments have the power to set tastes, and even then it is a risky business—witness the fate of the midiskirt.)

1. Draw a diagram of the market faced by a single firm in this industry (show both cost and revenue curves).
   a. Why does demand slope downward?

b. Is this demand curve more or less elastic than that for the whole industry? Explain.

2. Specify the profit-maximizing P and Q for this firm in the short run.

Show on the diagram the short-run profit of this firm.

3. Describe the process that leads to the "tangency solution" for this firm and show the resulting long-run P, Q, and profit.

a. Is this an equilibrium or a disequilibrium position for the firm? for the industry?

*b. Prove (mathematically or geometrically) that the long-run profit of a firm in the tangency position is zero.

4. Do you agree or disagree with the following: "Monopolistic competition is the most desirable form of industry structure because it has all the virtues of perfect competition and product variety besides."

PART IV.
Income distribution

33. Income distribution, taxation, and the issue of tax reform

During the 1972 Presidential campaign a great deal of attention was paid to the issue of "tax reform," in particular to the question of whether personal income tax rates in the United States are fair to lower- and middle-income citizens. Tax structures are classified as progressive, regressive, or proportional on the basis of whether the *percentage* of income paid in taxes increases, decreases, or remains constant as a taxpayer moves to higher income brackets. Personal income tax *rates* in the United States are progressive, ranging from a minimum of 14 percent to a maximum of 70 percent. If our tax system is based on the principle of "equal sacrifice,"

1. Why are our tax rates progressive (i.e., why doesn't everyone pay the same dollar amount)?
   a. What do progressive rates imply about the assumed marginal utility of income for individuals?
   b. What assumption about marginal utility of income is implied by equal dollar amounts?

  c. Can you think of a case in which it might be reasonable to assume an increasing marginal utility for income?

2. In an attempt to stem "taxpayer revolts" against ever-higher property taxation (claimed to be regressive), many state and local governments have turned to sales taxes as a major source of revenue.

  a. What's objectionable about regressive taxation?

  b. Does the switch to sales taxes solve the problem of regressivity? Why or why not?

3. By now it should be evident that the desirability of progressive, regressive, or proportional taxation depends on the assumption made about the *rate* at which the marginal utility of income declines. Which form of taxation would be implied for "equal sacrifice" by each of the three possible assumptions:

  a. Marginal utility of income declines at a *faster* rate than that at which income increases (for example, if income rises 1 percent the marginal utility of these additional dollars declines 2 percent).

  b. Marginal utility of income declines at a *slower* rate than that at which income increases.

  c. Marginal utility of income declines at the *same* rate as that at which income increases.

[You may now want to look back at your answer to question 1a.]

Which of these three assumptions seems most plausible to you?

Can you think of any way you could test or prove your assumption?

It is frequently argued that the progressive income tax in the United States is a device for redistributing income from upper- to lower-income groups, yet the pressure for tax reform in 1972 came primarily from the groups that would gain the most from such redistribution. This apparent paradox may be analyzed by examining the distribution of income in the United States over time.

4. Use the following data to plot Lorenz curves for the United States for the years 1910, 1965 (before tax), and 1965 (after tax). (Lorenz curves show the *cumulative* percentage of population plotted against the *cumulative* percentage of income they receive. Divergences from a 45° line measure the degree of inequality in income distribution. If you are not familiar with Lorenz curves, consult any standard principles text.)

SHARE OF MONEY INCOME RECEIVED BY FAMILY UNITS[a] IN THE UNITED STATES

Population Decile[b]	Percent of Income Received in		
	1910[c]	1965 (before tax)	1965 (after tax)
Lowest tenth	3.4%	0.9%	1.0%
2nd tenth	4.9	.5	2.6
3rd tenth	5.5	4.1	4.3
4th tenth	6.0	5.7	6.0
5th tenth	7.0	7.3	7.6
6th tenth	8.0	9.0	9.2
7th tenth	8.8	10.7	11.0
8th tenth	10.2	12.7	13.0
9th tenth	12.3	15.9	15.9
Highest tenth	33.9	31.2	29.4

[a]A single person or two or more persons related by blood or marriage living together.
[b]Determined by arranging all incomes from lowest to highest and dividing the list into tenths; each decile contains 10% of the population.
[c]There was no personal income tax in 1910.
SOURCES: U.S. Dept. of Commerce, *Statistical Abstract of the United States*, various years (Washington, D.C.: U.S. Bureau of Census), and B. A. Okner, *Income Distribution and the Federal Income Tax* (Ann Arbor: University of Michigan Institute of Public Administration, 1966), pp. 131–136.

a. What happened to the relative position of the poorest 40 percent of the population between 1910 and 1965? (Compare before-tax figures, since there was no personal income tax in 1910.)

b. If we define middle-income citizens as those (and *only* those) in the fifth, sixth, and seventh deciles, what happened to the relative position of this group in the total income distribution?

c. Now look at the *cumulative* effects for lower- and middle-income groups taken together on your Lorenz diagram. Can you explain from this why tax reform was a "coalition issue" in the 1972 campaign, appealing to both lower- and middle-income groups? Which deciles of the population *improved* their relative positions between 1910 and 1965? Who "paid" for these improvements (with relative declines) and in what proportions?

5. Do these changes discredit the progressive income tax in the United States as a redistributive device?

a. What other factors can you think of that might have influenced the pattern of income distribution since 1910?

b. In your opinion is the present degree of inequality in the United States income distribution undesirable? On what basis do you make your judgment?

6. If you regard the present distribution of income in the United States as undesirable,

a. Is the solution a more or a less progressive income tax structure? Explain your reasoning.

b. Is there some other solution you think would be more effective than changing the income tax rates?

c. Friedman has suggested that the progressive tax structure be replaced by a flat 23½ percent charge on all incomes regardless of size and without allowing any special deductions for anyone. He estimates that this would raise the same total revenue as the present, progressive system and eliminate the incentive to lobby for special favors and loopholes.[1]

1) Would this tax scheme be progressive, regressive, or proportional in *form*?

Do you think the effect of this tax scheme would be to make the *actual* distribution of income in the United States more or less equal than the *actual* 1965 distribution?

2) On the basis of what you've learned from your analysis, would you support or oppose Friedman's proposal? Why?

NOTES

1. B. A. Okner, *Income Distribution and the Federal Income Tax* (Ann Arbor: University of Michigan Institute of Public Administration, 1966), pp. 70–76. See also M. Friedman, *op. cit.*, pp. 191 ff.

34. Estimating the marginal utility of income—an introspective game

One drawback to the use of cardinal-utility concepts is the necessity of assuming that utility is somehow objectively measurable and comparable among individuals. (The classical utilitarians spoke of *utils* of pleasure or pain yielded to particular individuals by alternative policies or actions.) Von Neumann and Morgenstern have suggested a means of establishing an ordinal-utility index for a series of possible payoffs by finding the probability that would just induce an individual to accept an *uncertain* payoff (a gamble) rather than the *certain* receipt of a smaller amount.[1] Many television game shows are of this nature (e.g., "Let's Make a Deal"). The following problem is a chance for you to apply this method in estimating your own marginal utility of income.

Suppose that you are chosen from the audience to play a game that proceeds in a series of "rounds." In each round you have a choice between a *certain* (riskless) cash sum and one determined by drawing marbles from a box containing varying numbers of white and black marbles. There are no tricks or gimmicks involved. On the first round you are handed a $100 bill and told that you may keep it or gamble it on the result of a random drawing for a $1 movie ticket or a $500 stereo set. The drawing is made by pulling marbles from a box containing nine black marbles and one white one; black marbles represent movie tickets, the white one the stereo set.

1. What is the probability of drawing a movie ticket?
   What is the probability of drawing the stereo?
   What is the *expected money value* of the gamble?
   What is the expected money value of the $100 bill?
   If you are trying to maximize the expected money value of the game, will you accept the gamble or keep the $100?

2. Suppose, however, that you wish to maximize the *expected utility* (not money value) of the game. To do this you need to know the utility of each possible payoff. You can establish these utilities as follows:
   a. To determine the utility index of the $100 bill, let the utility of a $1 movie ticket = zero and the utility of the $500 stereo recorder = one.
      What is the expected utility of the gamble?
      What utility index of the $100 bill would make its expected utility just equal to the expected utility of the gamble?
   b. Would you personally be willing to take this gamble? If not, what would the probability of winning the $500 have to be to induce you to take the gamble? (Note: This is an introspective question; you cannot calculate an answer.)

The von Neumann-Morgenstern method uses the probability of winning the higher sum in the drawing as a measure or index of the utility attached to the $100 that must be risked to win.

3. Now suppose that the master of ceremonies hands you a second $100 bill and asks you to decide between your $200 in cash and the same gamble (movie ticket or stereo recorder).

   What probability of winning the stereo recorder would just induce you to risk your $200 on the gamble? (Your answer should be more than the probability you specified in question 2b but less than 1.0).

   a. Now repeat this question to yourself for cash amounts of $300, $400, and $500. Enter your answers, plus those from questions 2b and 3, in the following table:

Certain cash	Utility index	(= probability of winning $500 necessary for you to take the gamble)
$ 1		
100		
200		
300		
400		
500		

   b. Graph the data from your table.
   c. Using your graph, specify your marginal utility for successive $100 bills. Is it increasing, decreasing, or constant?

4. If such a graph were available for every individual, could valid interpersonal comparisons of individuals' utility indexes be made? (For example, would it be possible to *prove* that a progressive income tax results in more equal sacrifice of utility than proportional taxation or that public-housing programs increase total utility for society as a whole by transferring income from low- to high-marginal-utility individuals?)

5. Once you have worked out the utility indexes for an array of possible money values, you are equipped to make rational choices among a variety of gambles you might face. For example, consider

Gamble 1: .3 probability of winning $500 and .7 of winning $100

Gamble 2: .6 probability of winning $400 and .4 of winning nothing

a. If you want to maximize the expected *money* value of the game, which of the two gambles will you take?

b. If you want to maximize the expected *utility* of the game, which of the two gambles will you take?[2]

NOTES

1. J. Von Neumann and O. Morgenstern, *The Theory of Games and Economic Behavior* (Princeton, N.J.: Princeton University Press, 1944). See also F. Mosteller and P. Nogee, "An Experimental Measure of Utility," *JPE 59*, 5 (1951): 371–404.

2. The Bernoulli hypothesis is a special case of this general problem obtained when the probability of winning the gamble is .5 and the dollar amount of the payoff is doubled with every loss. It can be shown that unless some upper bound is stipulated the expected money value of this gamble will be infinite. See W. Nicholson, *Microeconomic Theory* (New York: Holt, Rinehart & Winston, 1972), pp. 149–152.

35. ZPG and the social cost of people

Population growth has long been of concern to economists. As early as 1798 Thomas Malthus noted that population growth had aggregate effects beyond those considered by individuals; more recently popular attention has been drawn to this issue by Paul Ehrlich and the Zero Population Growth (ZPG) movement.[1] ZPG can be viewed as an effort to make individuals aware of the social costs associated with individual decisions concerning family size and population growth. In its policy prescriptions ZPG has lent support to some of the demands of other groups such as Women's Liberation, whose positions are based on entirely different (individualistic) arguments.

1. The notion of a "population bomb" suggests a cumulative or compounding problem. Describe briefly the nature and consequences of the "explosion" that Malthus foresaw.

How does this differ from the modern concept of the nature and consequences of population growth?

2. Define *neighborhood effects.*

   What neighborhood effects are created by the decision of a couple to have a child? Does this depend on how many they already have?

   a. What *economic* motivation(s) might lead parents to have children? Would you expect these to be different in underdeveloped countries than in economically developed ones?

3. The Women's Liberation movement has recently advocated a general policy of free abortions on demand. Leaving aside the religious aspects of the issue, consider its economic aspects.

   a. Should abortion services be free (i.e., provided without charge to the "consumer")? Why or why not?

   b. How does your reasoning square with the implications of the neighborhood effects you've discussed in question 2?

   c. Suppose that it were argued that it is the *social* responsibility of the medical profession to provide abortion services free. Would you agree? Why or why not?

   Is there any difference between talking about the social responsibility of the medical profession and the social responsibility of, say, General Motors? Explain.

4. Can you describe a way in which the *market* mechanism could be used to limit population growth (i.e., to allocate children)?

   What would be the advantages and disadvantages of the scheme you've just described?

5. Do you think Malthus would have supported or opposed the ZPG movement? Contrast the Malthusian "solutions" to the population problem with the ZPG solution.

NOTES

1. Thomas Malthus, *An Essay on the Principle of Population* (1798) and Paul Ehrlich, *The Population Bomb* (New York: Ballantine, 1968).

2. P. A. Neher, "Peasants, Procreation, and Pensions," *AER 61*, 3 (June, 1971). Pt. I: 380–390.

PART V.
Public-sector
allocation

36. Parking prices—land rent and the allocation of urban space

Consider a city laid out as shown in Figure 17. There is one commercial garage (G) one block from the central business district (CBD) with 100 parking spaces. There are also 200 curbside spaces on city streets located as shown on the diagram; each of the five blocks can accommodate five cars on each side of the street. The garage charges 50c per hour and has no maximum time limit; city parking meters are currently set for a uniform charge of 10c per hour and are limited to a maximum time of one hour per space. All spaces, whether commercial or curbside, are priced by the hour (i.e., there are no monthly or weekly rates), and no overnight parking (between 6:00 P.M. and 8:00 A.M.) occurs anywhere. The garage owns the land on which it is located; it does not rent from the city. The city runs a bus line up and down each of the four streets to the CBD; the fare is 30c one way, and the full five-block ride takes ten minutes (or two minutes per block). Walking time is three minutes per block. Time spent either walking or riding is valued by citizens at 5c per minute.[1]

1. Define *economic rent*.

   Does the term *rent* apply only to payments for land, or can it apply, under the terms of your definition, to other factors?

   What is "quasirent" in Marshallian terms?

2. A survey commissioned by the city council reveals the following time distribution of parking in the city:

Hour	Total Number of Parkers	Number Parking in Commercial Garage
8:00	60	50
9:00	150	60
10:00	210	80
11:00	280	100
12:00	290	90
1:00	300	100
2:00	300	100
3:00	290	100
4:00	250	60
5:00	180	30
6:00	70	20

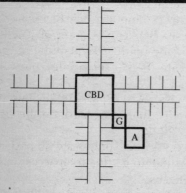

Figure 17. City with Central Business District and Parking Garage (Each Approach Street Is Five Blocks Long)

5. Suppose that a large office building that will bring 100 additional employees into the city every day is constructed on site A (see diagram).

   a. What effect would you anticipate that this would have on rates charged by the commercial garage? In what sense can these be called *monopoly rents*?

   b. Would you support a city council ordinance requiring this and all subsequent new office and commercial buildings to construct underground parking facilities for their own employees? What effect would such an ordinance have on the price of existing garage and street parking space? on traffic congestion in the CBD?

NOTES

1. For an empirical solution to a more complicated version of this problem, see S. A. Brown and T. A. Lambe, "Parking Prices in the Central Business District," *Socio-Economic Planning Sciences* 6, 2 (April, 1972): 133–144. An interesting insight into the practical politics of urban economics is provided in H. G. Manne, "The Parable of the Parking Lots," *The Public Interest*, 23 (Spring 1971): 10–15.

37. The economics of national parks (are they economical?)

The U.S. government owns hundreds of thousands of square miles of forest and timberland in the West and Northwest. Some of this has been developed into national parks equipped with campsites, trails, and ranger service, but much remains as virgin forest and is eyed longingly by lumbermen, resort developers, and others who argue that these natural resources are inefficiently allocated to park use. They cite as proof the fact that even when entrance fees are charged revenues do not cover the costs of park maintenance and operation, much less approach the commercial value of these natural resources. In essence they are bidding against park visitors for the use of these resources.

Suppose that you are asked to help determine a national policy for managing these lands "in the national interest." This means that you must consider the interests of those whose main concern is employment and income as well as those who argue for conservation and environmental values. Consider the situation of a single national park. Your research staff supplies a diagram (Figure 18) and tells you that it used the *willingness-to-pay principle* to estimate the demand curve for park facilities. A lumber company is offering the equivalent of $100,000 annually for the land and timber.

1. What is the willingness-to-pay principle? How, in practice, might you go about using it to estimate the points on the demand curve for park facilities?[1]
2. According to this demand curve, what is the total value park visitors would be willing to bid to keep the park?
3. If the park service is supposed to be a nonprofit operation with costs shown as ATC in Figure 18, what justifi-

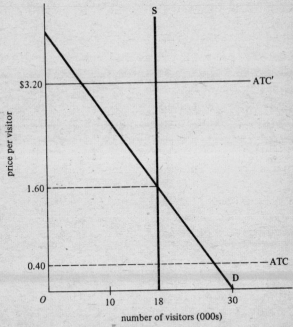

Figure 18. Estimated Demand for Services of Yosemite National Park as Park Land

cation, if any, can there be for charging an admission
fee greater than costs? Why charge any fee at all?

4. What is the *opportunity cost* of the park resources?

5. As a result of renewed interest in ecology and the
   natural environment, some of the most popular
   national parks have experienced overcrowding and
   pollution problems from trash and automobile traffic.[2]
   Campsites must be reserved in advance, and entrance
   fees have doubled.

   a. If the effect of these pressures has been to increase
      the costs of the park to ATC', can the park operation
      break even by discriminating its fees so as to charge
      $3.20 to the first 6,000 users and $1.60 to the re-
      maining 12,000 users?
      Could it break even if it could discriminate prices
      perfectly (i.e., charge each user the maximum price
      he is willing to pay)?

   b. Does this prove the charge that use of the land for a
      park is an inefficient allocation of natural resources?
      Some economists argue that *option demand* (the
      amount potential users would be willing to pay to
      keep open the option of visiting the park someday)
      ought to be included in the demand curve. How
      might the amount of the option demand be esti-
      mated? How would it affect the diagram?

      If it is valid to count option demand in establishing the
      value of a park, shouldn't it also be counted in calcu-
      lating the value of furniture that could be made from
      the park trees?

   c. If the lumber company's offer of $100,000 equals an
      average revenue per user of $4, what amount of
      subsidy is implied by a decision to continue
      operating the park at the break-even price of $3.20
      per user?

   d. What means other than entrance fees could be used
      to ration the use of park facilities?

What would be the distributional effects of each of these rationing methods? Which do you think would be the "fairest" way of rationing park use?[3]

6. What is a *public* (collective) *good*? How is it distinguished from a *private good*?

   Is the service provided by a national park a public or a private good?[4]

7. How would you respond to the charge that "ecology is a class-biased issue, the luxury concern of those middle- and upper-class Americans who have succeeded economically by exploiting the same natural resources they now seek to deny to others as a means of competing for their share of the national wealth."

NOTES

1. M. Clawson, *Economics of Outdoor Recreation* (Baltimore: Johns Hopkins Press, 1966) and *Methods of Measuring the Demand for and Value of Outdoor Recreation* (Washington, D.C.: Resources for the Future, 1959).

2. See the report of the federally sponsored Conservation Foundation Study, "National Parks for the Future," which recommends banning automobiles and related services from national parks (reported in *New York Times*, September 17, 1972, p. 1).

3. Note that a similar line of argument can be applied to the creation and maintenance of park areas on valuable property in urban areas.

4. B. A. Weisbrod, "Collective Consumption Services of Individual-Consumption Goods," *QJE 78*, 3 (August, 1964): 471–477 and M. Friedman, *op. cit.*, pp. 31 ff.

38. A slick problem of social cost

Several times in recent years oil wells drilled in the ocean floor off the California coast have "blown," releasing thousands of tons of crude oil into the ocean that have eventually washed up on California beaches. This has produced demands by conservation groups that the Department of the Interior prohibit offshore drilling. In response, F. L. Hartley, president of the Union Oil Company, has said: "We should not fall prey to the beautification extremists who have no sense of economic reality."[1]

Leaving aside the emotional aspects of the issue, discuss the hard *economic* factors involved in the following way:

1. Give a careful definition of *social cost.*
   How is this different from private cost?
2. What is the difference, if any, between the social and private costs of a barrel of offshore oil? (List as specifically as possible the items that would fall into each category of costs.)

Use this distinction to explain why it may be said that the petroleum industry tends to "overproduce" crude oil.

3. One class of antipollution policies would impose the full cost of pollution wholly on the polluter.

Would prohibiting all offshore drilling be a policy of this kind?

Give the advantages and disadvantages of such a policy.[2]

4. Explain in Galbraithian terms why the Department of the Interior has been slow to take any action to regulate the oil companies in this case.

5. Show how the concepts of *Pareto optimum* and the *compensation principle* apply to this case.

6. It has been argued by some analysts that pollution problems really stem from a legal problem of property ownership: Since no one really *owns* collective resources like the air and the beaches, there is often no injured party interested in protecting the resource to bring suit against polluters. In such cases it is suggested that the solution lies in creating property rights in these resources so that those who protect and enjoy the beaches for recreation can exclude those who would use them for other purposes.[3]

On July 24, 1972 the New Jersey Supreme Court ruled that "the public trust doctrine dictates that the beach and the ocean waters must be open to all on equal terms and without preference."[4] This ruling makes it illegal for municipalities along the shore to limit access to their beaches to their own residents, whose taxes pay for the upkeep of those beaches.

a. What effect do you think this ruling will have on the general upkeep of the beaches?

b. Do you think the ruling will make policies of the type described in question 3 (imposing the costs of pollution directly on the polluter) more or less attractive?

c. Do you think a change in property ownership laws
could be an effective solution to the problem of pollution of California beaches?

NOTES

1. *New York Times*, April 26, 1969.

2. See R. A. Coase, "The Problem of Social Cost," *Journal of Law
and Economics 3* (October, 1960) and a rebuttal by W. Baumol, "On
Taxation and the Control of Externalities," *AER 62*, 3 (June, 1972):
307–322.

3. See, for example, J. H. Dales, *Pollution, Property & Prices*
(Toronto: University of Toronto Press, 1968); C. Reich, "The New
Property," *Yale Law Journal 73*, 5 (April, 1964): C. Reich, "The New
Wolozin, "Environmental Quality as Government Largess," *National
Tax Journal 24*, 4 (December, 1971) 501–505.

4. *New York Times*, July 30, 1972, p. E2.

39. A case of "pure" profit?

The New York Times of February 15, 1970 carried the following statement:

> *Administration officials have been crying with one voice that antipollution costs are properly a "cost of doing business" and thus can be passed on to the consumer. But industrialists and those in Congress attentive to their views do not see the matter in quite such simple terms. They fear there is a limit to what the consumer will bear and when that limit is reached, the remaining antipollution costs will be reflected in lower corporate profits.*
>
> *Furthermore, they contend that costs which big companies and new efficient plants can possibly absorb become insupportable for small companies and old plants. The upshot, they say, may be unemployment with accompanying outcries from local government, especially in small towns where a plant is a principal employer.*

Comment on this by answering the following:

1. What are social costs?
   Are these the same as the "antipollution costs" referred
   to in the statement? If not, make the distinction clear.
2. Which of these (social costs, antipollution costs) consti-
   tutes a "cost of doing business"? or do *both*?
3. Analyze the difference of opinion between the administration and businessmen over whether antipollution costs can be passed on to the consumer.
   a. Who is right? What does this depend on?
   b. Is the administration's position an argument for or
      against imposing the full costs of pollution directly
      on the polluter?
4. What would an economist say about the argument put
   forward in the second paragraph of the statement from
   an efficiency standpoint?
   What other criteria (other than efficiency) might be
   used to evaluate that argument?

40. The economics of law enforcement

In recent federal and local political campaigns, candidates have made promises to spend more on "law and order" a primary issue. The popularity of law and order as a winning campaign issue might be thought to imply that society has been spending less than an optimal amount of its resources on law enforcement. Others argue that not the total but the *distribution* of expenditures is unbalanced—too much is spent on "victimless" crimes and too little attention given to more serious crimes against person and property.[1] It is possible to analyze law enforcement as a service provided at a cost in real resources by the community for the benefit of its citizens.

1. Why is law enforcement provided as a public rather than a private good?
2. How are the real resource costs of enforcement distributed among citizens?
   How would the costs of nonenforcement be distributed among citizens?

Suppose you are the captain of a small-city police force and need to determine the optimal allocation of your enforcement resources, which consist of 10 men and $100,000. You have only two major problems to which you must assign men: enforcement of the laws against possession and sale of marijuana, and a rising tide of automobile thefts. The current situation is as follows:

Present Resource Allocation	Number of Convictions per 100 crimes	Estimated Average Loss per Offense
Marijuana: 5 men ($50,000)	17	$1000
Auto theft: 5 men ($50,000)	21	$3500

For simplicity make the following assumptions:

1. Policemen can be used in either assignment at the same cost.
2. Auto thefts are committed only for income (i.e., thieves take no pleasure in crime for its own sake).
3. Marijuana users do not steal autos; this is largely the work of professional syndicates. Marijuana, being non-addictive, is not financed by other forms of street crime.

You will find it helpful to enter your calculations for the following questions in the accompanying table (page 141).

3. What is the probability of detection for each crime? What is the probability of nondetection ("success") for each crime?
   Note that the probability of detection increases with the number of crimes committed by an individual, so that the probability of at least one conviction in n crimes is $1 - (1 - p)^n$ where p is the original probability of detection for the first offense.

4. From the information given in the table, calculate the total penalty for each auto theft.

TABLE 1. SCHEDULE OF PENALTIES AND PROBABILITIES FOR AUTO THEFT

Offense	Fine	Jail and Years	Total $value	Penalty	Probability of Detection(p)	Success(1−p)
		Legal Penalty				
1st	$500	0 or ½	$	$		
2nd	1000	1 or 2				
3rd	2000	1 or 2 or 3				

(Assume that the average car thief values one year in jail at $10,000, the price he would require to "take the rap" for someone else.)

5. What is the *expected gain* (EG) from committing the first car theft? the second? the third?
   What is the *expected loss* (EL) for the first offense? the second? the third?

6. If car thieves are rational "businessmen," how many thefts will each commit if the courts customarily assign only minimum jail sentences (in addition to the fine)? What would be the maximum number of stolen cars you would anticipate if every one of the city's 65 car thieves were rational in this way?

7. What effect, if any, would there be on the total number of stolen cars if penalties were increased to the *maximum* for each offense (with no change in arrest or conviction rates)?

8. As police captain you have two strategies open to you for fighting auto theft: (a) You can increase the number of men assigned to the apprehension and conviction of car thieves; (b) you can increase the penalties by prosecuting for the maximum penalty in each case and pressuring the courts and legislators to increase legal penalties.

   a. Explain briefly how each of these activities would affect your calculations in questions 5, 6, and 7.

   b. How high would the total penalty for a first offense have to be to make *any* auto theft an irrational undertaking?

      If the fine stayed the same, how much would the maximum jail sentence have to be increased to discourage all car theft?

It is generally recognized that trying to raise the penalties for an offense is a rather inefficient way for police to fight crime. A more direct method is to reallocate existing law enforcement resources and/or to increase the total enforcement budget (usually at the expense of some other category of public expenditure).

9. a. What rule should be applied to determine whether the existing allocation of enforcement resources is optimal or not?

      Using the information you've developed so far, what evidence is there that the existing resource allocation is not optimal? How should resources be reallocated?

   b. Many law enforcement agencies try to maximize their total number of arrests and convictions. Explain why this leads to nonoptimal allocation of law enforcement resources.

10. How should the city decide whether to use the new tax revenues it expects next year to enlarge the total law enforcement budget or to increase public-school expenditures?

NOTES

1. A. B. Smith and H. Pollack, "Crimes Without Victims," *Case & Comment 77*, 4 (July–August, 1972): 9–15. See also G. Stigler, "The Optimum Enforcement of Laws," *JPE 78*, 3 (May–June, 1970): 526–536; G. Becker, "Crime and Punishment: An Economic Approach," *JPE 76*, 2 (March–April, 1968): 169–217; T. R. Ireland, "Optimal Enforcement of Laws: A Comment," *JPE 80*, 2 (March–April, 1972): 421; M. Katzman, "The Economics of Defense Against Crime in the Streets," *Land Economics 44*, 4 (November, 1968): 431–440 and I. Ehrlich, "Participation in Illegitimate Activities: A Theoretical and Empirical Investigation," *JPE 81*, 3 (May/June 1973): 521–565.

41. A welfare analysis of the draft versus a volunteer army

Alternative ways of staffing the armed forces may be evaluated more precisely by using the tools of welfare analysis.[1] Consider the system of random draft by lottery as opposed to an all-volunteer system, using Figure 19 for reference.

V_3 = total number of draft-eligible men
V_2 = draft quota established by the Pentagon
V_1 = number of volunteers at the current pay rate, P_1
P_1 = private's pay of $2160 per year. (For simplicity assume that all draftees enter as privates and that all privates are paid at the same rate regardless of length of service.)

The supply of volunteers slopes upward, reflecting the belief that the number of volunteers is responsive to changes in the pay scale.

Demand is perfectly inelastic, reflecting the call under a draft system for a fixed number of men regardless of price.

(Later we will use an elastic demand curve to reflect the fact that under an all-volunteer scheme the number of men called will be a function of their price.)

1. How many additional men must be procured either by draft or by pay-inducement?
   Calculate this requirement as a percentage of the total of eligible nonvolunteers.
2. What increment in the basic pay rate would be required to fill the quota *without* conscription?
3. What is the total taxpayer (government) cost if the additional men required to fill the quota are drafted? if they are "bought" without conscription?

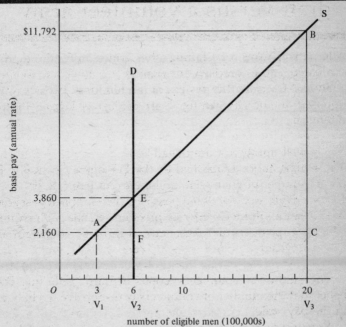

Figure 19. Market for Military Manpower Under the Draft

4. What, then, is the *tax value of the draft* to the public (i.e., how much does the public save by using the draft rather than a market system of recruitment?)

5. However, we must compare with this *gain* to the taxpayers the welfare *loss* imposed on individuals drafted against their will. You can estimate this welfare loss in the following steps:

   a. The total draft-eligible pool of men is $(V_3 - V_1)$. If every one of these were drafted, what would be the *draftees' total welfare loss*?

   b. Now suppose that the required percentage of these men (from question 1) is selected by random lottery to receive draft notices. What is the proportional welfare loss attributable to these draftees.[2]

   c. Suppose now, however, that we can select the draftees so as to take only the men with the lowest welfare loss (i.e., $V_2 - V_1$). What is *their* welfare loss?

   d. What is the *net cost* of using a random rather than a selective recruitment process?

6. Now express this net cost of the random draft as a ratio to the tax value of the draft (which you calculated in question 4).

   a. It may be argued that when this ratio is less than one a draft system is an efficient means of staffing the armed forces, whereas when the ratio is greater than one a selective recruitment process ought to be used. Explain.

   b. Can you prove that as the required manpower quota approaches 100 percent of all those eligible the draft becomes a more efficient way to fill this quota? [That is, prove that as the quota requirement approaches 100 percent the net cost of the draft (from question 5d) declines.]

7. Policy problem: We have now established that for relatively low manpower quotas a selective scheme of recruitment is more efficient than the draft. How, in

practice, can we devise a selective scheme that will attract into service only those with the lowest opportunity costs (i.e., $V_2 - V_1$)? In its 1970 report the President's Commission on an All-Volunteer Armed Force recommended that the necessary manpower be bid for in the open market by raising the basic pay rate from $180 to $315 per month.

Will this be enough to recruit the necessary number of volunteers (consult Figure 19)?[3]

8. Suppose now that on the basis of your analysis the government accepts the all-volunteer proposal.

Show the effect of this on the diagram.

Mark the new equilibrium point H and indicate the new equilibrium price and quantity as P_m and Q_m.

9. The term *welfare* has been used in a very specific way throughout this analysis. Define this economic interpretation of the term and indicate what other factors you might want to include in a more comprehensive concept of welfare, or welfare loss, associated with the draft.

NOTES

1. This problem is adapted from E. F. Renshaw, *op. cit.* For a view of the draft from the individual's standpoint, see chap. 15 of this book.

2. J. R. Davis and N. A. Palomba, *op. cit.*

3. For a contrasting view see M. Janowitz, *op. cit.*

42. Benefit-cost analysis— marginalism in the public sector

Benefit-cost analysis is an extension of the principle of marginalism to the sphere of public expenditures.[1] Instead of equating the marginal cost and marginal revenue from an incremental dollar or unit of output, it seeks to balance the total benefits and costs, properly adjusted, of an incremental project or program in the government budget. It is a particularly useful technique for evaluating "lumpy" (indivisible) investments of considerable size such as a hydroelectric dam, an urban renewal project, or a highway extension.

Suppose that you are asked by the mayor of a large city to analyze a proposed high-speed bypass to be built around the central part of the city. The proposal includes the following specific conditions:

We propose to build a four-mile limited-access bypass around the city to carry through traffic and ease the congestion of downtown streets. It is estimated that construction will take one year and that the capacity of the finished highway will be adequate for ten years thereafter.[2] *Estimated construction costs will include (1) value of land and demolished structures: $150,000; (2) materials and overhead: $100,000; (3) labor cost (wages): $300,000. In addition, engineering and geological surveys will cost $50,000, and operating and maintenance costs are estimated to amount to $300,000 spread evenly over the ten-year life of the project. Residential property values in the immediate vicinity of the bypass can be expected to decline by about $75,000. It is proposed that the project be financed with a local bond issue for $150,000 at 5 percent for ten years, with the balance of the capital construction costs covered by a federal grant from the Department of Transportation. The current rate of interest being charged by commercial banks to prime customers is 6 percent. A toll of 25c would be charged for use of the full four-mile section or any part thereof.*

The anticipated effects of the project are as follows: The bypass will be used for an estimated 800,000 car trips per year, 550,000 of which will be diverted from downtown streets and the remainder ("new traffic") generated by the existence of the highway itself. For those diverted from city streets, an estimated time saving of 20 minutes per trip will result; we estimate the value of travel time at 5c per minute. In addition, benefits will accrue to downtown merchants and shoppers from faster movement in and out of the central business district (an estimated time saving of about 10 minutes per trip) and to inner-city residents from reduction of auto emission levels now produced at the rate of 10 grams of carbon oxides per average crosstown trip. It is estimated that these pollutants have a minimum cost of 2c per gram in terms of health and maintenance effects imposed on others. The current volume of city traffic is 850,000 trips per year. To the extent that downtown traffic congestion is reduced, we would anticipate further benefits in the form of fewer accidents and faster bus and commercial delivery service.

Making the working assumptions that all benefits are distributed evenly over the life of the project and that the numerical estimates given in the proposal are accurate, analyze the proposed project by answering the following questions:

1. Set up the benefit-cost balance sheet for the highway project, showing anticipated benefits on the left and costs on the right. (Note: All items given in the proposal do not necessarily have to appear in the balance sheet. Remember that you want to estimate total *social* benefits and costs of the project, not just its commercial profitability.)

2. On a separate page show your calculations for the money value of each item and enter these figures in the balance sheet. Be careful to discount both benefits and costs, where necessary, to get the *present value* of both benefits and costs associated with the bypass. (Hint: You will find it useful to use a compound-interest table for this.)
   a. What is the purpose of discounting?
   b. Explain your choice of discount rate.
   c. What additional effects (benefits or costs), if any, do you think should be included in the balance sheet? Indicate how you might measure these effects in dollars if this is possible.

3. Using just the items given in the original proposal (i.e., excluding for the moment any entries you've added in question 2c—these will be picked up later),
   a. Calculate the *net benefits* of the highway project, its *benefit-cost ratio*, and its *internal rate of return*.
   b. Which of these is the best indicator to the city highway department of whether or not it should undertake the project?
   c. Which is of the greatest interest to the mayor and the city comptroller, who must allocate the overall city budget?
   d. Would you advise the mayor to approve or disapprove the project? Explain your reasoning.

Now take into consideration any additions you made under question 2c. How, if at all, do these change your recommendation to the mayor?

4. What difference, if any, would it make in your answer to question 3a if the city's $150,000 were to be paid directly from current tax revenues instead of from the sale of bonds? (You don't need to recalculate the precise figures if you can explain clearly the *direction* of change in the indexes.)

   a. Should interest paid on bonds be counted as a cost, a benefit, or neither? Explain.
   b. What difference, if any, would it make in your answer to question 3b if labor for the highway were drawn from a pool of unemployed construction workers?

5. Suppose that you now learn that under the law highways built with federal funding cannot charge tolls. Would this change your final recommendation to the mayor? Explain.

6. What are the major *redistributive effects* of the project on residents of the metropolitan area likely to be as between (a) rich and poor, and (b) city and suburbs?

NOTES

1. Benefit-cost analysis is sometimes distinguished from cost effectiveness and PPBS (planning-programming-budgeting systems). Benefit-cost analysis is used to determine whether a project should be undertaken and how it ranks in comparison with other expenditures directed toward the same goals; cost effectiveness (used by the Department of Defense) seeks to minimize the cost of a project already settled on for other reasons; and PPBS is a method of incorporating the regular evaluation of benefits and costs of a department or agency into its administrative operations, especially the budgetary process.

Benefit-cost analysis has been used to evaluate programs in urban renewal, population control, airport location, polio research, mosquito control, defense, and water resources. An overview of basic benefit-cost literature through 1965 is available in A. R. Prest and R. Turvey, "Cost-Benefit Analysis: A Survey," *Economic Journal* 75, 300 (December, 1965). See also A. Maas, "Benefit-Cost Analysis: Its Relevance to Public Investment Decisions," *QJE 80*, 2 (May, 1966) and J. Mao, "Efficiency in Public Urban Renewal Expenditures," *JAIP 32*, 2 (March, 1966).

2. In reality both the construction time and the project life would be longer. Shorter periods and smaller dollar amounts are used here to reduce the number of necessary computations.

43. The CIA and Soviet GNP (or, the treachery of index numbers)

You are a CIA agent assigned to "debrief" a student who has just returned from a year of study in the U.S.S.R. The CIA has estimated that the productivity of the Russian economy will equal that of the United States by the year 2000 and is anxious to know how accurate its estimate has been so far. You are able to learn only the following information from the student:

U.S.S.R. PRODUCTION AND PRICES

	P_{50}	Q_{50}	P_{57}	Q_{57}	P_{70}	Q_{70}
Bread	$ 0.10	1000	$ 0.20	1500	$ 0.30	2000
Steel	50.00	100	60.00	200	40.00	500
Shoes	2.00	500	2.00	600	2.00	700
Autos	500.00	2	400.00	3	300.00	4

U.S.S.R.

GNP, 1950: $265
GNP, 1970: $620

In addition, you know:

U.S.

GNP, 1950: $285   CPI,[1] 1950:   84.0 (1957 = 100)
GNP, 1970: $740   CPI, 1970: 113.0

From this information prepare your report, including

1. *Absolute* real growth of the U.S. economy: $ ——, or
   —— percent.
   Absolute real growth of the U.S.S.R. economy: $ ——,
   or —— percent.
2. How accurate has the CIA estimate been so far?
   (Show all calculations and explain your reasoning. Be
   sure to note any sources of bias and important assumptions on which your calculations and conclusions rest.)
3. Which country has the higher standard of living?

NOTES

1. The CPI (Consumer Price Index) is of the Laspeyres form (base
year weights) calculated on a 1957 base. It includes only consumer
goods.

44. The rising cost of college

A freshman at Cornell University in 1932 recorded his annual expenses as follows:[1]

	P_{32}	Q_{32}	In 1972 they were:	P_{72}	Q_{72}
Tuition	$300.00	1		$3000.00	1
Meals	0.75	400		1.75	400
Books/supplies	5.00	10		10.00	50
Room	200.00	1		800.00	1

He is now contemplating sending his son to Cornell and needs to know

  1. How much has the *real* cost of a Cornell education increased over this period? ———— percent.

His son is also considering Colgate, which lists the following expenses.

	P_{32}	Q_{32}	P_{72}	Q_{72}
Tuition	$300.00	1	$2855.00	1
Meals	0.50	400	1.75	400
Books/supplies	5.00	10	15.00	10
Room	150.00	1	600.00	1

2. Which school was cheaper in terms of its *current* cost in 1972?

   Cornell: $ ____   Colgate: $ ____

3. Which school had the greater increase in its expenses between 1932 and 1972?

   Cornell: ____ percent   Colgate: ____ percent

4. *Average* annual increase in costs over the 40 years at

   Cornell: ____ percent   Colgate: ____ percent

5. Assuming that these *average* rates will continue for the next four years, which school would require the greater *total* outlay? (Assume that 1972 was the student's freshman year.)

   Total four-year expense at Cornell: $____
   Total four-year expense at Colgate: $____

6. What is the index number problem?
   What is its solution?

NOTES

1. 1970 figures from *Cornell University General Information and Announcements 1972–1973*, pp. 73–75 and *Colgate University Catalogue 1971–1972*, p. 27.

Glossary of useful mathematical and graphic relationships

The following are a few of the relationships most commonly used in microeconomic analysis. If you do not understand the derivation of a concept, you should review the appropriate section of any standard microtheory textbook. No attempt is made to give derivations or proofs here.

1. *Total* revenue, cost, profit, or utility is the average price, cost, profit, or utility times the total number of units ($P \cdot Q$, $ATC \cdot Q$, etc.). Graphically, the total is the area of the rectangle whose base is a specified quantity and whose height is the vertical distance from the abscissa at that quantity to the point of intersection with the average revenue, cost, profit, or utility curve. As an alternative the total can be measured as the whole area under the *marginal* revenue, cost, or profit curve up to a specified quantity. For example in Figure 20 total cost at Q_1 may be measured by the distance BL, the area OP_1FQ_1, or the area $OGDQ_1$. (When $Q = 0$,

ATC and MC are really infinitely large. Therefore point G may be thought of as the values of ATC and MC when Q is a very tiny amount, not quite zero.)

2. *Marginal* revenue, cost, or profit is the *additional* revenue, cost, or profit attributable to an incremental unit ($\Delta TR/\Delta Q = TR_2-TR_1/Q_2-Q_1$, etc.). Graphically marginal value is measured by the slope of the tangent drawn to the relevant total curve at the specified quantity or by the difference between the areas of two

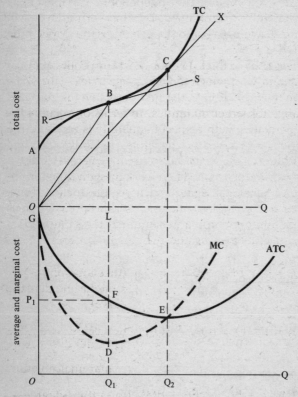

Figure 20. Graphic Relationships Among Total, Average, and Marginal Costs on Arithmetic Scale

"total" rectangles. In terms of calculus it is the first derivative of the total function with respect to quantity (dTR/dQ, dTC/dQ, etc.). In Figure 20 marginal cost for Q_1 is DQ_1, or the slope of the tangent RS.

3. *Average* revenue, cost, or profit is total revenue, cost, or profit divided by the specified quantity (TR/Q, TC/C, etc.). Graphically an average value can be measured by the slope of a ray from the origin to a point on the relevant total curve at the specified quantity. Recall that the slope of a demand curve is $\Delta Q/\Delta P$ even though the independent variable, P, is conveniently diagrammed on the vertical axis. In Figure 20 average cost for Q_1 is FQ_1, or the slope of the ray OB.

4. *Maximization* of total revenue, cost, or profit occurs at the quantity for which the marginal value (= the slope of the total function = the first derivative) is zero and negative for larger quantities. In terms of calculus the first derivative with respect to quantity is zero and the second derivative is negative ($dTR/dQ = 0$ *and* $ddTR/ddQ < 0$). *Minimization* occurs where $dTR/dQ = 0$ *and* $ddTR/ddQ > 0$. When working with functions in three-dimensional space, such as production functions, it is possible to have a "saddle point" that is both a minimum and a maximum at the same time.

5. Some useful *functions* and their *derivatives* are:

   a. $Q_d = a - bP$; $\dfrac{dQ_d}{dP} = -b$ (the slope of a straight-line demand curve)

   b. $TR = P \cdot Q = (Q^2_d - aQ_d)/-b$; $\dfrac{dTR}{dQ} = \dfrac{a - 2Q_d}{b}$

   (= marginal revenue)

   c. $TC = a + bQ - cQ^2 + dQ^3$ (for a third-degree curve like that in Figure 20);

$$\frac{dTC}{dQ} = b - 2cQ + 3dQ^2 \ (= \text{marginal cost})$$

d. $\log x$; $\dfrac{d \log x}{dx} = 1/x$ (= Bernoulli form of marginal-utility function)

6. Elasticity of demand = $\dfrac{\Delta Q_d}{\Delta P} \cdot \dfrac{P}{Q_d}$. Graphically, elasticity can be measured on a straight-line demand curve by the ratio of the lower to the upper portions of the demand curve at a specified point. If the demand function is curvilinear, draw a tangent to it at the relevant point and proceed as before. Other elasticities (income, cross-, supply, substitution) are calculated analogously.

7. *Arithmetic scale*—Equal linear distances represent equal *absolute* amounts.

   Logarithmic scale—equal linear distances represent equal *percentage* amounts.

   Semilog scale—uses arithmetic scaling on the horizontal and logarithmic scaling on the vertical axis. Semilog scaling is most commonly used to show percentage changes in a magnitude (log scale) over time (arithmetic scale). A straight line on a semilog scale represents a constant (compound) *rate* of change over time.

8. *Probabilities*—The probability of getting any specified number, 1 through 6, on one toss of a die is 1/6 or, more generally, x (= number of "winning" outcomes)/ N (= number of possible outcomes). The chance of getting a specified outcome *at least* once in n tries is $1 - (1 - x/N)^n$ where x/N = probability of winning once, $(1 - x/N)$ = probability of losing once, $(1 - x/N)^n$ = probability of losing at least once in n tries, and $1 - (1 - x/N)^n$ = probability of winning at least once in n tries.

9. *Expected value* is the probability of an event occurring multiplied by its nominal value. For example, the expected value of $100 won by rolling a 5 in one toss of the die is 1/6($100) = $16.66. In some instances a

probability may be a subjective rather than an objective estimate.

10. *Compounding, discounting, present value and internal rate of return*—The value of $1 compounded at rate i for n years $= \$1(1 + i)^n$ where i is expressed in decimal terms (i.e., 5 percent $= .05$). $1 compounded at 5 percent for 10 years is $\$1(1.05)^{10} = \$1(1.629) = \$1.63$. Discounting is the inverse of compounding; $1 received 10 years from now is worth how much today? $\$1/(1 + i)^{10} = \$1/(1.05)^{10} = \$1/(1.629) = \$0.614$; $0.614 is the *present value* of $1 received 10 years hence. Compound-interest and present-value tables are available in almost any statistics book. For quick reference the following equivalences are useful:

$1 at   5 percent doubles in about 14½ years
$1 at   7 percent doubles in exactly 10 years
$1 at 10 percent doubles in about 7½ years

The *internal rate of return* is a special case of discounting; it is the discount rate that makes the present value of benefits = the present value of costs of an investment (or makes the *net* present value of the project = 0).

C

75 76 7 6 5 4 3 2